# THE JEWISH QUARTERLY

The Jewish Quarterly is published four times a year
by The Jewish Quarterly Pty Ltd
Publisher: Morry Schwartz

ISBN 9781922517012 E-ISBN 9781743821909
ISSN 0449010X E-ISSN 23262516



Subscriptions 1 year print & digital (4 issues): $74.99 AUD | £42 GBP |
$56 USD. 1 year digital only: $44.99 AUD | £25 GBP | $32 USD.
Payment may be made by Mastercard, Visa, or by cheque made out to
Schwartz Books Pty Ltd. Payment includes postage and handling.

To subscribe, fill out the form in this issue,  subscribe online at
jewishquarterly.com, email subscribe@jewishquarterly.com or call 1800 077 514 /
+61 3 9486 0288. Correspondence should be addressed to:  The Editor,
The Jewish Quarterly, Level 1, 221 Drummond St, Carlton VIC 3053 Australia
Phone 61 3 9486 0288 Email enquiries@jewishquarterly.com

Editor: Jonathan Pearlman. Associate Editor: Jo Rosenberg.
Literary Editor: Natasha Lehrer. Contributing Editors: Ian Black and
Jo Glanville. Publicity: Pitch Projects. Sales and Marketing Manager:
Caraline Douglas. Management: Elisabeth Young. Marketing and Editorial
Assistant: Michelle Wenig. Design: John Warwicker and Tristan Main.
Production: Marilyn de Castro. Typesetting: Tristan Main.

Issue 245, August 2021

# THE JEWISH QUARTERLY

# Contributors

**Nir Baram** is an award-winning Israeli author and journalist. His latest novel is *At Night's End*.

**Nancy Berliner** is the Wu Tung Senior Curator of Chinese Art at the Museum of Fine Arts in Boston, Massachusetts.

**Jessica Cohen** is a translator who has worked with leading Israeli writers. Her translation of David Grossman's *A Horse Walks into a Bar* won the Man Booker International Prize.

**Lina Khatib** is the director of the Middle East and North Africa Programme at Chatham House.

**Deborah Levy** is a British playwright, novelist and poet. Her books include *Swimming Home, Hot Milk* and, most recently, *The Man Who Saw Everything*.

**Elie Podeh** is Professor of Islamic and Middle East Studies at the Hebrew University of Jerusalem. His book about Israel's secret relations with Middle East states will be published in 2021.

**Anne Sebba** is the author of *Les Parisiennes*, winner of the 2016 Franco-British Society Book Prize. Her latest book is *Ethel Rosenberg: An American Tragedy*.

**Magda Teter** is Professor of History and the Shvidler Chair in Judaic Studies at Fordham University. Her most recent book is *Blood Libel: On the Trail of an Antisemitic Myth*.

# After Oslo

## *A farewell to peace*

## Nir Baram
### (translated by Jessica Cohen)

When Israel signed normalisation agreements with the United Arab Emirates and Bahrain at the White House, there was little enthusiasm among the Israeli left. Prime Minister Benjamin Netanyahu had just declared a national lockdown to curb the spread of Covid-19. The occasion also marked the final collapse of the Israeli progressive camp's long-held conviction that the Israeli–Palestinian conflict was the catalyst of Middle East tensions, and that only its resolution could effect peace in the region.

Recent decades have shed light upon the obvious truth: hostilities in the Middle East are only marginally related to Israel. The region is rife with conflicts that date back far before the establishment of the State of Israel. Moreover, the Arab states no longer view their ties with Israel through an Israel–Palestine lens. Egypt long ago circumvented the Palestinian quandary when it signed the Camp David Accords in 1978, and by 2020 there was general indifference toward the conflict, as evident in the Gulf states' policies.

For most Israelis, the White House ceremony and the subsequent thronging of Israelis to Dubai – for both business and pleasure – was a funeral for the focal point of Israeli politics since the mid-1980s. Here was further evidence that the Palestinians do not hold the only key to rapprochement between Israel and the Arab world. From a utilitarian viewpoint, if not a moral one, the Israeli right wing had chalked up a win.

And then came the devastating spring of 2021, with another round of hostilities, which reminded us of the plain truth: Palestinians and Jews still live here, permanently intermingled, and twenty years from now there will be 25 million of them, divided roughly equally between the two nations. What will life look like then, without a resolution, without equal rights, with most Palestinians still under Israeli occupation? Israelis have stopped asking these questions. They seem too distant, too vague, and most of the risks posed by a failure to solve the conflict have ostensibly receded. In 2021 we learned once again, however, that the conflict is always here, even if most Israelis are able to ignore it in between escalations. With the Hamas regime in Gaza, and constant tensions at the holy sites in Jerusalem, these waves of violence will not end.

One Saturday during the war, my son and I went to the beach. Kids were playing in the water, running at the waves. It was the picture of serenity, until I paid attention to the children's voices: they were pretending that the waves were rockets from Gaza, screaming, "You won't fall on Israel!" as they kicked them. I felt a crushing sense of failure when I realised that this was the reality our children are inheriting from us.

How did we get here?

## *After the trenches*

My father and I are driving on the Jerusalem–Tel Aviv highway. The country is under curfew because of the pandemic, and the roads are deserted. Hardly anyone is at the gas stations, and the few people we do see hurry by, their faces masked. If we get stopped by the police, it's going to be hard to justify our excursion. My father, Uzi Baram, is eighty-two. He became a member of the Knesset in 1977, in the elections known in Israel as "the upheaval", when Likud first took power after three decades of Labor governments. In 1992, he was appointed minister under Yitzhak Rabin.

These evening drives, which have no clear destination, have become a custom. The driving makes us feel a little better, easing the suffocation of lockdown. Sometimes we stop at the Jerusalem Forest or in any open space where you can see the stars. My father says it's important to remember that there are stars in the sky.

"Remember how you once told me that I was born after the Yom Kippur War because it was fashionable to have kids then?" I ask him.

"Yes. It was considered a patriotic act."

"Because of all the dead?"

"Because lots of people died, yes."

"Where were you in the Yom Kippur War, in '73?"

"I'll tell you something: even though I was close to government circles, the war came as a complete surprise to me. I was called up for reserve duty, and we went off to the Sinai Desert. We ran into an Israeli battalion emerging from the battlefield, and the soldiers were a wreck. I remember the smell of Israeli tanks burning. If you'd asked me a week before that, I'd have told you aliens would land on Earth before the Egyptians could trounce Israeli armoured units."

"What was your political response to that war?"

"You don't respond immediately. You gradually come to grasp that things you viewed as unequivocal reality were in fact unfounded assumptions. For example, the Arab states' military weakness compared to our enormous power. All of a sudden, new questions arise."

"What else changed after the war?"

"Before the war, we – Mapai, the workers' party – had total control of the country. After the war, something fundamental was undermined. The certainty that we knew how to run the country was called into doubt, both internally and by our adversaries. The fact that Arab armies had surprised us was not just a total failure, but a fracture in the reality of our lives."

"Yes, a lot has been said about that failure," I reply. "But did anything else come out of the trenches?"

"Yes," my father says, "and this is interesting: what emerged from the war was that many people, soldiers, had seen their friends die. They experienced great personal loss, but they also lost their trust in the state institutions. As secretary of the Labor Party in Jerusalem at the time, I sat with these men after the war and listened to them. There was a lot of anger, but I started to notice that they were talking about something that to me seemed impossible, almost utopian: we had to make peace and finally put an end to the wars."

"Would you say that's where your political calling began?"

"It wasn't immediate. But in our generation, the political left started to cohere in the mid-'70s. The Yom Kippur War soldiers were several years younger than me, but we all shared the sense that clout was not policy. Remember that thousands of people had died in the war, and the grief in Israel was immense. We suddenly had to ask ourselves if the country could pay such a heavy price in yet more wars. To me it was very clear that we could not."

"So what solutions were offered?" I ask.

"There weren't any real solutions in the mainstream centre-left yet. The two-state notion was only mentioned in the far left, at the time, but a centre-left camp was coalescing around the idea of reconciling with the Palestinians and ending the occupation. Peace Now was founded and garnered a lot of support. In retrospect, you could say that we started to get closer to the two-state model."

"How did the Labor Party's old guard respond?"

"They weren't there yet. Not Rabin, not Golda Meir, and not really Peres either."

"Your father was a Mapai man, a minister in the first Rabin government. You could say he was a member of the state's founding generation. How did he see things?" I ask.

*Suddenly the country had changed, as had the borders of our lives*

"He didn't believe in any of that. Thought it was a big fantasy. 'Who are you going to make peace with?' he asked. 'The PLO? Yasser Arafat? They kill civilians, they hijack planes, they want to destroy us.'"

After taking my father home, I drove along the empty streets of Tel Aviv, where the silence and darkness seemed eerily similar to my childhood nightmares. As I drove, something else occurred to me: in 1967, the Labor Party reached the height of its power, and yet the party was murky on its goals. After the Six-Day War victory, it was clear that the State of Israel was here to stay. The existential fear had abated; the party's greatest mission – founding and establishing a Jewish state – was complete. As a consequence, religious Zionism began to push for Jewish sovereignty over the biblical "Land of Israel". Secular Zionism did not quite know how to contend with this notion in the early years. Rabin, Peres and others in the Labor Party turned a blind eye and even authorised a number of settlements. The irony of the 1973 war, which shattered faith in the Labor Party, was that the new central tenet of the secular centre-left began to emerge at its margins: the division of the land between Jews and Palestinians. The concept crawled towards the centre in the late 1970s and early '80s, but the decisive impetus arrived in 1987.

## The Intifada

While I was writing my last novel, *At Night's End*, I thought of a scene that has been burned in my memory since 1988: it's a Saturday afternoon, we're hanging out at the schoolyard, and a few local kids, now soldiers, are home for the weekend. They're serving in the occupied territories, where they've been sent to quash the Intifada – the Palestinian uprising that started at the end of 1987. Until recently, these muscular, bronzed young men were just like us, playing soccer, spending evenings at the shopping centre. Now they have returned from an unknown land where a war of sorts is being waged. They don't talk much, but the stories spread: they get Molotov cocktails thrown at them, they have fireproof uniforms, they use sticks to beat Palestinians who curse at them, they're not afraid of anything.

The First Intifada fell on us like a meteorite off its course. Before the uprising, we could not even put the problem into words. And then suddenly the country had changed, as had the borders of our lives. East Jerusalem was now a place we didn't go near. Too dangerous. At school they didn't explain why this had happened. We knew very little about the Palestinians from our textbooks: there were Arabs and there were Jews, and the Arabs had always wanted to destroy us. Our parents talked about it a little more, but before the Intifada we'd never really listened.

When I was in the sixth grade, my school held a mock election ahead of the 1988 national vote. A group of us put together a Labor Party list, with Likud as our rival. We held conventions in the gym at recess, and the Intifada was a fixture of our speeches. Even though the minister of defense, Yitzhak Rabin (a Labor Party man), was a hardliner who spoke of "breaking the Palestinians' hands and feet", we, like our parents, talked of peaceful solutions.

For the younger generation of the Israeli left, the Intifada was evidence that the political solution they'd begun advocating was critical. It proved that you could not oppress another people – men, women and children – without paying a heavy price. And the toll was not only moral but involved human lives, both Israeli and Palestinian. We believed that unless there was peace with the Palestinians, Israelis would have to live with incessant violence and our society would become morally corrupt, as would the army fighting a civilian population that included children. At school, our position was that only dialogue between the two sides could alter the violent reality. One fact became crystal clear to my generation: the Israeli–Palestinian question was the primary issue facing our country. The school elections were turbulent, and our camp eked out a slim victory. In the real elections, Likud narrowly prevailed.

The Intifada accelerated our political maturation and focused it on the Israeli–Palestinian question. Scenes of Palestinian kids handcuffed and blindfolded, terrorist attacks in Israel, soldiers coming back from the territories – it suddenly felt very close, and we were forced to acknowledge that there was a nation in our midst that was willing to take on the Israeli army in its fight for freedom. Was it possible for Israel to step out of the cycle of bloodshed and make peace?

## In the schoolyard

Thirty-odd years later, I'm back in the schoolyard in Beit HaKerem, the Jerusalem neighbourhood where I grew up. A voting centre is set up for the 2020 elections, but there's not much excitement outside: a few signs, a handful of tired young people handing out pamphlets. I approach a group canvassing for Labor and Meretz, the two leftist parties that collectively swept roughly 40 per cent of the votes in 1988. If they're lucky, they may achieve 4 per cent in 2020. I ask why they're here.

"We get paid 300 *shekels* a day, plus lunch and dinner," one of them explains. "You can't make that kind of money anywhere else." They're all around eighteen years old, just before their military service.

"You're working for left-wing parties. Are you on the left?"

"No way! Are you crazy? What's the matter with you? We're working because they pay us."

"So you're right-wingers?"

"No, not really," they answer. "We're in the centre."

I ask what voting issues interest them.

"Security. We don't want any more terrorist attacks." Also: "Don't let the Haredim take over our lives." Another adds: "The economy. The only jobs we can get pay terribly, that's why we're here. We make a killing on election day. If only there were elections every day."

"Are you concerned about the conflict with the Palestinians?"

They give me slightly puzzled looks. "There's nothing going on with that now," one says. "No attacks, not much fuss, they live their lives and we live ours."

"But there's no solution yet," I point out. "We're still living here together."

"Fine, but people tried to solve it and they couldn't, right? They dealt with that for a century. And then things went crazy and buses were blowing up all the time, loads of people died. Now there isn't anything really urgent about it. Talk to us when things heat up again. Until then, we have our own problems to worry about."

"What kind of problems?"

"We all work like dogs, we'll never be able to afford our own apartments, everything's hand to mouth, everything's expensive in this place. Anyone whose parents don't have assets, apartments, that kind of stuff, is totally screwed. We don't believe anyone, they're all corrupt. And now you turn up asking about the Palestinians – who cares about that?"

I ask them what they think the Israeli left wants.

"To get rid of Bibi."

"What else?"

They seem stumped.

"And what does the right want?" I ask.

"They want us to be strong, not give in to anyone, and no more bombs going off."

I hang around with them a while longer. There is something infectious about their glee, their laughter. Oddly, though we're twenty-five years apart in age, I know their humour and their language. The way the boys always poke fun at each other's little weaknesses, and talk about girls; even the nicknames they give each other are familiar. But when it comes to politics, we grew up in two different countries. There is no resemblance between my political consciousness and theirs. Not even a point of overlap.

Perhaps the main reason for this is that they were born after the era of peace, which means they have no memories of the mood during the early Oslo years – the hopefulness, the ceremonies, the excitement, the faith. They were born into the failure, in an age when hopes for peace had been dashed and the reality of the conflict seemed unalterable. I can spend hours arguing about the Israeli–Palestinian conflict with right-wingers of my generation: we both view it as a critical issue. But these young people have only ever known an unsolvable conflict that occasionally erupts into violence. They are far removed from the left wing because it offers no approach that interests them – it's not even on their political map. And because they believe, perhaps influenced by their parents or by the history they know, that leftist policies lead to instability.

## The first left-wing government

Yitzhak Rabin rose to power in 1992, partly as a result of the terrorist knife attacks occurring throughout Israel. The biggest public uproar erupted after a fifteen-year-old girl, Helena Rapp, was stabbed to death in Bat Yam, a suburb south of Tel Aviv. Violent protesters took to the streets for days, and many Israelis felt that the Likud government was failing to protect them. Rabin promised to negotiate an end to the violence with the Palestinians. As minister of defense, he had overseen the suppression of the First Intifada, and although he'd taken a hardline approach that had garnered widespread criticism from the left, he'd come to believe that Israel could not continue to forcefully control the Palestinians.

The elections represented an intoxicating triumph for the Israeli left, with Labor regaining power after fifteen years, and the newly formed left-wing alliance party, Meretz, winning twelve seats and joining the coalition government. But was it truly a Labor victory?

Dan Hasson is a Jerusalem-born architect, roughly my age. We met after moving to Tel Aviv, but we've both retained a lot of our Jerusalemite traits. Tel Aviv and Jerusalem are very different cities in almost every respect, certainly politically. Unlike many Tel

Avivians who grew up in left-leaning neighbourhoods and hardly ever encountered different viewpoints, we Jerusalem lefties rubbed shoulders with right-wingers from a young age: we went to school with them, played with them, partied with them. The right wing was not something amorphous, and so we had a greater awareness of its various nuances.

Hasson is a political man who regularly takes part in protests. As an architect, he is involved in various initiatives addressing the effects of the occupation on the ground, and he has been observing Israeli politics for many years. We walk along the Tel Aviv beach on a summer evening, laughing about our childhood days, when a trip to the sea was like travelling to a foreign country. When I bring up the Labor Party's 1992 win, he says something that sounds illogical:

"The Labor Party didn't regain power in 1992."

"Remember the euphoria? There was going to be a new world ..."

"What do you mean? Of course it did," I counter.

"No. The Labor Party that controlled Israel until 1977 – they used to be Mapai – that party was a nationalist, militarist, centrist party with socialist sympathies, far removed from any ideas of peace and reconciliation. The party led by Ben-Gurion and Golda Meir, and a young Rabin, did not believe that the Jewish–Arab conflict could be resolved in our lifetime. Whereas the party that formed a government in 1992 was something completely different."

"Then how would you define the party that won in 1992?"

"It was the Labor Party by name, but it was nothing like Mapai. In fact, it was a reaction to Mapai. They were politically moderate and extremely capitalist. A new entity, really. It was the first party with left-wing politics to win an election in Israel, and it formed the first left-wing government in Israel. Maybe the only one."

"Interesting. So it was essentially a new party with a familiar name."

"Exactly. The young generation, people who were affected by the Yom Kippur War, were solidly on the left, and now for the first time they held power, which allowed them to implement their plans: making peace with the Palestinians and partitioning the country."

"But Rabin and Peres were older. A completely different generation."

"Yes," Hasson concurs, "but Rabin and Peres were influenced by that generation. It's no coincidence that the people who set up the secret Oslo negotiation channels – Yossi Beilin, Uri Savir, Ron Pundak and others – were precisely from the generation whose views were moulded by the Yom Kippur War. Oslo wasn't Rabin's idea, after all, but he sanctioned it and, ultimately, he understood that it was something momentous."

"That's true," I say. "In that sense, the Rabin government fulfilled its mandate."

"Yes. It made big strides towards solving the conflict. In fact, you could look at it this way: the generation of Yom Kippur War soldiers gave the older generation a little push to take dramatic steps in solving the conflict: talking to the PLO, withdrawing from the Gaza Strip and Jericho. And their biggest accomplishment? They managed to persuade most of the country, which viewed Arafat as the devil incarnate, that the idea of land for peace – and not just that, but giving land to the PLO – was a sound one. Today people can't appreciate it, but that was a sea change in Israeli society: roughly 55 per cent of the public supported the Oslo Accords. They were willing to give up land."

"That was also the first collaboration between the Jewish left and the Arab left, which effectively propped up the Rabin government."

"Yes, the peace project created a uniform goal among the Jewish and Arab left for the first time. Everyone viewed peace with the Palestinians as the main objective. That's why the Arab parties were essentially part of Rabin's coalition, and that's why it was a rare political moment."

"We were high schoolers then, and we were the greatest believers."

"We had no doubts," Hasson says. "Remember the euphoria? They put out televisions in my school so we could watch the peace accords being signed."

"Mine too."

"There was going to be a new world ..."

## *The protester*

When I grew up in Beit HaKerem, the neighborhood was home to civil servants, journalists and other professionals. It was hard to see the sky through the lush green treetops that lined the streets. One morning in 1995, when I was seventeen, I woke up at around six to calls and shouts from outside. At first I couldn't make out the words, but then I realised people were yelling, "Wake up! Your peace is killing us!" I looked out the window and saw a group of young people standing outside our apartment building, waving signs and calling for the Rabin government to resign. Twenty-five years later, I'm sitting on the steps outside my old building, looking up at the balconies. I wonder if anyone I know still lives here, and I start to think about death, as I do whenever I come back here. A thin, bearded man in his thirties comes over and stops.

I recognise him: "You protested here once, remember?"

"Of course," he says, "I went to a million demonstrations. When I think of the '90s, I think of protests."

"How old were you back then?"

"Around fourteen."

His name is Guy Yifrach, and today he is deputy mayor of Ma'ale Adumim, a huge settlement near Jerusalem that is considered by mainstream Israelis to be just another Israeli city.

"When the Oslo process began, you were a kid. How did you view it?"

"I was against it right from the start," Yifrach says. "Not just because we lived in Ma'ale Adumim and my parents were Likud people, but because Labor wanted to split up the country. We realised you were aiming for a Palestinian state that would be led by terrorists like Yasser Arafat."

"But when you demonstrated here, it was because of the terrorist attacks, not because of the basic premise of Oslo."

"Same thing. There were horrible terrorist attacks going on while the peace process was supposed to be happening. So where exactly was the peace? Rabin's government wouldn't let anything stop it, like there *had* to be peace. And that's not true: you can't just believe in peace and ignore the reality of people's lives."

"It's true, there were attacks. But you oppose the notion of partitioning the country in principle. Many Israelis gave Oslo a chance, but the terrorism changed their minds. Maybe you took advantage of that?"

"What do you mean, took advantage? Weren't there constant terrorist attacks? It's true, though, that with or without terrorism, we objected in principle. The Jewish people have a profound connection to this space, historically and religiously. We objected to dividing the land into two states and, on top of that, giving Arafat and his terrorists power and legitimacy. I mean, it was obvious that at some point they would turn against us. But we also saw what was happening around us. Did Labor really expect the public to understand that there was a peace process while buses were being blown up?"

"You're right," I admit, "we agree on that. The public could not accept peace with terrorism."

"But there's something else that still resonates today. Since at least '77, there's been a clear war between the old Labor Party elite and the newer, more right-wing and Mizrahi forces. The peace process was a story told by the old elites, not by us. The 'peace elite', helped by the media, put on a massive campaign to persuade the country that peace was the future. And anyone who didn't enthusiastically accept that future was living in the past, too religious, too Jewish, too hateful. That was something we felt very strongly."

> *"It's not set in stone that there has to be a practical plan for every problem"*

"And now Likud has been in power for many years. You won. Do you have a plan?"

"Sometimes there's no plan. It's not set in stone that there has to be a practical plan for every problem. That's the thing you may not have understood. Palestinians and Israelis live in the same space, and I want peace too, but when the left wing's peace efforts failed, Israelis concluded that you can't solve this conflict. That, in fact, every time left-wing governments tried to solve it, we ended up with chaos and instability."

"How do you explain the decline of the Israeli left? When you came here to protest, the leftist parties had a lot of power."

"Because back then, the left had a clear direction, even if I thought it was the wrong one. What is the left today? What does it propose? Going back to the '90s? What is the positivist definition of the Israeli left today? Other than calling Netanyahu corrupt all day long?"

After Yifrach leaves, I remember a scene from our 1988 school elections that embodied a division even more explosive than responses to the Intifada. On the first day of our campaign, all the kids in our year gathered in the schoolyard, and the teacher asked us to split up according to political affiliations: Likud on the right, Labor on the left. Almost every single Mizrahi student moved to the right, and practically all the Ashkenazi students to the left. It was a clear-cut divide that told a very profound story about Israeli society. But no one at school talked about it.

## Back to high school

A few years after those 1988 elections, I started high school at Le'Yad Ha'Universita, a prestigious school widely known by Jerusalemites as Leyada. One of my classmates was Yifat Elhayani, who came from a Sephardic family and had excelled at elementary school. Leyada had instituted what they called projects, where kids from disadvantaged backgrounds were diverted into separate classes. In the school administrators' view, integrating the project kids with the other students would only underscore the disparities between them and lead to frustration. The segregation was clear even in the physical locations of the classrooms. Most of the project students were Mizrahi, and most of the regular students were Ashkenazi. Yifat and I were close in high school; her brother used to tease me about being in love with her.

Today Yifat is a supervisor at the Ministry of Education. We meet outside the school. Not much has changed, including the contrast between the sun-drenched courtyard and the ugly grey square building.

"I remember that when I came to Leyada, I was kind of shocked when I realised what my status was," Yifat recalls. "I was a 'project', not good enough to be in the regular classes. The separation was unmistakable. Once, I even stood up at a class assembly and said: 'Look at us. We're not ghosts here. We also go to this school.'"

"Yes, I remember that."

"On the other hand, we had our pride. We didn't want to be like the kids in the regular classes. They seemed boring to us."

"That's because most of them were," I quip. "What's your memory of the Oslo Accords?"

"There was crazy enthusiasm about it in school. They put televisions outside and everyone watched the ceremony. It was hard not to get caught up in the euphoria."

"How did the kids in your class respond?"

"They were less enthusiastic. Most of us came from right-wing homes. It felt like all that had nothing to do with us. But I was actually a little different. I was influenced by what was going on in the country at the time, and even though my family voted Likud, I started reading *Haaretz*. I even joined the youth division of Meretz."

"What was your impression of the left?"

"Maybe it was about fitting in, connecting with kids from your classes. But when I was young, I gave the idea of peace with the Palestinians a chance. In Meretz they were always talking about peace and human rights and democracy. But there was one issue: the kids from our school who were in Meretz always said really nice things, but when it came to their own school they didn't even see us, they didn't see how we were like second-class citizens. I wanted to tell them: *Take a look at your own school!* That really discouraged me."

"So when did you give up on peace?"

"I was never really on board with the idea. From home I believed in Greater Israel, maybe even as a sort of religious notion. But Oslo swept me up, all the excitement, especially at school. You guys had this confidence in it, so much faith and optimism. And then all the bus bombings started, and we were afraid to take the bus but it was the only way we could get around. That sent me back to Likud. In 1996, when Peres ran against Netanyahu, I voted for Netanyahu, and I've voted Likud ever since."

"Did those hopeful days leave any imprint on you?"

"A little. I was kind of a sceptic, but willing to give it a chance."

"If the peace process had worked, could you have supported giving back land? Despite your parents' opinions and your feelings about Greater Israel?"

"Yes," Yifat replied, "I would have supported that."

"What is the left wing today, in your view?"

"Today? Something marginal. Something that used to exist."

## *"The left is practically heresy"*

The decades-long alliance between the Labor Party and the country's Haredim (the ultra-Orthodox) began when the state was founded. Despite Labor's secularism, many of its leaders, including David Ben-Gurion, had used a Biblical narrative to justify the establishment of the Jewish state. After the 1977 upheaval, the Haredim joined forces with the victorious Likud, and by the 1980s it was clear that the Haredi positions on national policy were secondary to their desire to form a coalition with whichever of the two major parties won the election. The Haredim had become the kingmakers of Israeli politics. After that, everything changed.

Shas, the party that primarily represents Mizrahi Haredim, reluctantly joined Rabin's coalition government in 1992, hoping to preserve the allocation of state funds to its private education system, but withdrew after little over a year. In 1999, Shas joined Ehud Barak's short-lived coalition. As a consequence of the left wing's steps towards peace, the Haredi population – both Ashkenazi and Mizrahi – came out against partitioning the land, rejected agreements with the Palestinians and essentially aligned itself with the right wing. Starting in the late '90s, the Haredim began openly supporting Likud, which had always been perceived as closer to Jewish tradition than Labor. Today this seems like an obvious partnership, but at the time it was a dramatic shift.

> *The Haredim had become the kingmakers of Israeli politics*

On municipal election day in Jerusalem, I walk around some of the Haredi neighbourhoods. Things are quite different here compared with the secular neighbourhoods I visited earlier, where you would barely know it was election day. Hordes of excited yeshiva students are everywhere, cars with blaring loudspeakers urge people to go out and vote "for Torah's sake". The streets are littered with election pamphlets.

I approach a large group of yeshiva students. They are very young, perhaps twenty. "Are you a lefty?" they ask, eyeing me warily. But when we start talking, their suspicions fade. They're used to being attacked by secular people demanding to know why they don't serve in the army. But I have a different question. There used to be an alliance between the left and the Haredim, I remind them.

"It's true," they say, "there was an alliance. Our leaders and the left wing's leaders were often on the same page."

So I ask them: "Why do you think the alliance ended? Can it be restored?"

"When Labor goes back to being what it used to be – respecting the Jewish religion, being strong on security, caring about Jews and not just Arabs – then we'll talk," replies one young man.

"Don't be ridiculous," another man scolds him. "They do care about Jews, it's just that the left has become radical, both on secular-religious issues and on regional politics. How can we support them when they want a totally secular state that has nothing to do with Jewish values, and they enter partnerships with the Arabs?"

Seemingly unaware of the absurdity, another explains: "When the left goes back to being in the centre, like it used to be, maybe there can be an alliance between us again."

"Come on," I protest, "you know very well that Labor was willing to do a lot to form an alliance with you. They proposed religious legislation that Likud wouldn't have dreamed of. That's not the problem, it's something deeper."

One man sums it up: "Look at the country over the past few years. Overall, the situation is good, things are being managed. There aren't any big adventures like Labor had with Oslo. The right wing is better suited to running the country, that's clear."

"The right wing brought back security, didn't it?" says his friend. "There are no more terrorist attacks. You're too busy with human rights, Arabs, that kind of thing. This isn't the left of Ben-Gurion and Rabin."

I follow them to the Shas headquarters, an impressive operation buzzing with action. I ask them: "Do you really support

Netanyahu? He's a secular, Ashkenazi Zionist. You're not any of those things – where does this support come from?"

"It's because the left keeps persecuting him. He's running things pretty well, he cares about the Jewish people and about Judaism, he's liked all over the world, and the left hounds him. They're full of hatred. Of all the secular leaders, he's the one closest to us. He respects us and our religion, and he believes in showing strength."

*

Yisrael Grubeis, a young Haredi journalist, is considered a prodigy. He belongs to the Gur sect, one of the largest and strictest Hasidic dynasties. At twenty-seven, he has eight children. Unlike many Haredim, Grubeis takes an interest in secular culture, and is particularly fond of Thomas Mann and Dostoevsky. We meet one day for a walk in the Jerusalem Forest. Surrounded by nature, we encounter no one else on the quiet, shady paths.

"Can't you invite me to your neighbourhood?" I tease him. "Are you embarrassed by our friendship?"

Grubeis laughs. "I'm not embarrassed at all, but socialising with a secular writer would be frowned upon in our yeshiva. Perhaps one day I'll invite you to a lesson."

I recount what the yeshiva students told me on election day, and I ask about the alliance between the left and the Haredim.

"I think you should ask yourself what the Israeli left actually is," Grubeis responds. "To me, the left wing is a substitute for religion. Meaning, it's a different value system. Assimilation and lack of conservatism are far closer to the left than to the right. When the Haredim enter an alliance with the left, there are two reasons: either the left is in power and then there's no choice, or the left is so weak that it won't be able to achieve anything."

"As a Haredi," I ask him, "what is it about left-wing values that you find particularly threatening?"

"For example, human rights at any cost, equality among human beings, marriage between a Jewish woman and a non-Jewish man: these are dangerous values. They threaten our future as a Jewish society. There is no Haredi way to accept the principle that all humans are equal. To us, they're not."

"So my aspiration to equality between Jews and Arabs threatens you?"

"When I listen carefully to what you're saying, yes, it threatens me. It could lead to a non-Jewish state. In my opinion, the whole left wing is a sort of attempt to evade a painful question …"

"The question of why are we here?"

"Exactly. You secular leftists have no real justification for confronting the Palestinians. I can confront them and say: this is ours because of God. But you – what will you say? This is a historical process?"

I agree, more or less.

"That's exactly your problem. The difference between the secular right and the secular left, in my view, is that one is a desire and the other is an opinion. The leftist position is an opinion: it has a value system that's the opposite of religion, it focuses on individual rights and universal values of equality. And that is why, to us, it's almost heresy."

I have to laugh at his definition. "Why do you say it's *almost* heresy?"

"Because I'm a polite young man. Anyway, compared with the left, the secular right in Israel represents a simple idea, an innate desire for assets, territory, a home, Jewish tradition, conservatism. These are the values a person is born with, and Haredim identify with them. The secular right, unlike the left, does not present a value system that threatens the Jewish faith and our way of life, and that's why we're with them. The right wing was always the natural home for the Haredim, it's just that in the Mapai era it was beneficial to us to get along with them."

## *Children of Oslo*

A few Palestinian kids pass us on the street, giggling and chatting, closely followed by a group of Jewish kids. The looks in their eyes are similar: slightly bored, slightly defiant, looking for action. The two groups are close, but they might as well be living in different worlds.

I'm walking to East Jerusalem with Nivin Sanduka, a 37-year-old Palestinian woman who grew up in the East Jerusalem neighbourhood of Shuafat and went to an all-girls school near Damascus Gate. We stand on the border between West and East Jerusalem. I tell Sanduka about the soldiers coming back to our schoolyard when I was a kid, and ask about her most vivid memory from the First Intifada.

Hers is also from school. There were frequent confrontations between Israeli soldiers and Palestinians at Damascus Gate, and she remembers soldiers on horseback galloping into their schoolyard and the girls running into the classrooms, hiding under benches as the smell of teargas lingered in the air.

Sanduka and I grew up not far from each other. Our experiences were completely different, of course, but when we talk about the '90s and the Oslo Accords, there do seem to be some common elements. She remembers the exhilaration, with people spilling out onto the main road in Shuafat, some throwing flowers at Israeli buses, and national Palestinian songs blaring. "We were convinced that there was finally going to be peace," she recalls. "That things were going in the right direction. But the younger generation has no memory of that hopefulness."

These are exactly my own realisations. "So in some ways, despite the huge differences, we are both children of Oslo."

Sanduka laughs. "Exactly. There was a moment when we were there, in the hope for peace."

West Jerusalem has changed in recent years. There is now a noticeable Palestinian presence. You hear Arabic in cafés; shoppers of both religions try on clothes at the same mirrors in the same shops. These may sound like trivial scenes, but they did not exist when I was growing up.

Sanduka confirms that she got to know West Jerusalem after the Oslo Accords, when she was amazed to discover the tree-lined neighbourhoods, boulevards and parks. West Jerusalem looked like Europe to her. Ironically, it was in that "era of peace" that she became aware of the huge gaps between Jews and Arabs. I wonder when she first realised that there probably would not be peace.

"When all the bus bombings were going on, in 1996. I was already hanging around West Jerusalem then, and I started feeling afraid. After all, I could be killed in an explosion. And I saw that the settlements were still being built; lots of Palestinians couldn't find work in Israel, even after Oslo, and things weren't changing at the pace they'd promised. Today I have a different understanding of things. Palestinians now view Oslo as one big trap."

After the failure of the Camp David peace summit with the Palestinians, in 2000, the Second Intifada broke out. Israel responded in full force to the violent Palestinian resistance, resulting in many casualties on both sides. That, Sanduka says, was predictable.

I point out that most left-wing Israelis were surprised.

Sanduka responds: "There were restrictions on freedom of movement, the settlements were growing, the Palestinian Authority had let down a lot of Palestinians. There was despair and a depressed economy, and then the summit failed."

"Do you understand what happened to the Israeli left in the Second Intifada?"

"Not really."

"Are you interested in the question?"

She considers for a moment, then smiles. "Maybe."

I outline how the Second Intifada, and Ehud Barak's declaration that there was no Palestinian partner to peace, destroyed widespread Israeli support for the process.

> *"We haven't really been able to rehabilitate the 'peace camp' on either side"*

"That also made us stop believing that we had a partner for peace," Nivin says. "In the '90s, despite the bombings and the killings, we met lots of Jewish Israelis who talked about peace, and as soon as the Second Intifada began, almost all of them simply vanished. Palestinians could not understand where the Jewish supporters of peace had gone."

"I'll tell you where they went: many of them stopped believing in peace. They had to explain to other people and to themselves what had happened. Most of them didn't really understand ordinary Palestinians' perspective. They couldn't see that the '90s had given Palestinians big hopes and ended in huge disappointment. For many peace-supporting Israelis, it was an awakening: here was Arafat, encouraging terrorism and fear. This was exactly what the right wing had been saying. There was a sense that the right was vindicated."

"But where were the Jewish peace supporters?" Nivin insists.

"They fled, from both the bombings and the peace process. I think this political moment we're talking about, in 2001, was one of the most significant in the whole Palestinian–Israeli story, because we're still paying the price for it today. We haven't really been able to rehabilitate the 'peace camp' on either side."

She agrees: "Today, a Palestinian who collaborates with Israelis, even with peace supporters, is accused of collaborating with normalisation – meaning, normalising the status quo."

"They're absolutely right, but without that it's hard to make progress."

"Yes. And we've been stuck in the same cycle this whole time. Twenty years. It's pretty amazing."

## Next to the wall

After meeting Nivin, I take the winding road to Jericho and turn off towards Ras Khamis and Ras Shehada, Palestinian neighbourhoods on the other side of the separation wall. There, I enter a different world. The landscape looks familiar: a row of tall buildings behind a wall, smoke curling up from fires lit on the street, but unlike Shuafat, where Nivin lives, these neighbourhoods are under neither Israeli nor Palestinian rule. It's a de facto no man's land. I've visited here many times, mostly because I found it hard to believe that there are neighbourhoods so close to the centre of Jerusalem where there are no police, no roads and no trees, and the air is thick with the smell of burning rubbish. Ras Khamis and Ras Shehada are part of Jerusalem according to law and geography, but the separation wall built by Israel has cut them off from the city.

Near the wall, I meet Ismail, a tall sixty-year-old with white hair and a smooth, boyish face. He served time in an Israeli prison, and is now a community activist. I've been to his house a few times, but today he says it would be best to meet outside. I don't ask why; some questions are better left unasked. I do ask if there's any new information about the murder of Baha Nabata.

"How many times are you going to ask the same question?" Ismail says. "There's no information and there's not going to be."

I knew Baha quite well, having toured the area with him a number of times. He was an impressive, eloquent young man, a neighbourhood leader who worked to improve children's futures and protect residents' rights. He had two children. Baha and I often stood together on the garbage heaps and talked about the future and the urgent need for improvement in these neighbourhoods, and how to raise awareness in Israel. Baha was murdered near his home a few years ago, shot by an unknown assailant on a motorcycle, in the middle of a bustling street. I've often thought of him since then. When we used to talk, his despair was always mingled with a glimmer of hope. He needed to believe that the neighbourhoods could be brought back from the brink of chaos. His death remains unsolved, unexplained. The police conducted a token investigation, and it was clear that the murder was connected to local Palestinian rivalries.

*When you visit these places, the grand ideas seem to trickle through your fingers*

For me there was something particularly demoralising about Baha's death, even more so than all the big events. Not only because I liked him and was sad to lose him, but because the murder sharpened my sense that all the talk about the conflict and the two-state solution becomes meaningless when you get to know the West Bank and East Jerusalem and realise how fragmented they are. Each region and each city has its own rules of movement, its own local leadership, its own enigmatic rivalries. When you visit these places, the grand ideas seem to trickle through your fingers.

I ask Ismail about Baha's wife and children, and he tells me, perhaps without meaning to, that Baha's brother was murdered a few weeks ago. No one knows why. Unsurprisingly, no arrests have been made.

I ask no more questions – I know the answers anyway – but just look at the spot where Baha and I stood a few years ago. I knew back then that in a few hours I would be going home to Tel Aviv while he would stay here, raising his kids in the contaminated air.

Ismail and I hug silently, and I watch him walk back to the checkpoint. We used to spend hours discussing the conflict, but now our talk of Oslo and solutions and history – the same topics that came up with Nivin Sanduka – seems very distant. Almost naive. Lately, it feels as if there's nothing left to say.

## The 2020 protests

The second pandemic lockdown in Israel, in late September 2020, was no longer met with compliance. Israelis were more tired, more impoverished, more desperate. In fact, I've never seen Israel in such a state of despair. After Netanyahu imposed restrictions that prevented the weekly demonstrations outside his official residence in Jerusalem, people stood holding signs on street corners near their homes. Interestingly, this new form of protest swept up a lot of Israelis, young and old, who had never gone out to protest before. Yet polls showed gains for Naftali Bennett's Yamina ("Rightwards") alliance, which is further to the right of Netanyahu on almost every issue. In other words, even with Netanyahu's failure to manage the pandemic and salvage the economy, even with a seemingly unnecessary lockdown, millions of children stuck at home and hundreds of thousands of newly unemployed and impoverished Israelis, the left-wing parties still did not gain support. On the contrary.

I'm driving to Caesarea with my five-year-old son, Daniel. It's against the regulations, but I want him to play on the beach with friends. The roads are empty. I'm a little afraid of being stopped by the police, but determined to let Daniel see the water. Witnessing his delight as he runs on the sand and splashes in the waves is worth it.

When we head back to Tel Aviv in the late afternoon, we drive past a street-corner demonstration. Daniel wants to stop: he's only five, but he knows about the protest movement and has learned to yell "Bibi go home!" We park and walk over to the young protestors. Most of them are waving black flags. I ask them to explain the rally.

"We're out here to protest Netanyahu's corruption and failures. He's devastated Israeli society. We want him gone."

"And then what?" I ask.

"Then we'll get a different leader, someone less corrupt, and maybe the country can start to heal. We can't live with Netanyahu anymore. We don't believe a word he says."

I ask if they are on the left.

"Yes, more or less," answers a young man whose t-shirt says "Netanyahu, go already".

"What will the left do if it gains power?"

"There'll be more welfare, less corruption, someone will look out for us. The whole atmosphere will change."

"But those are things everyone promises. Is there some idea that will really make a change?"

"First Netanyahu needs to leave, then we'll see."

"What if he's replaced by a different right-winger, someone even more extreme?"

"Even that would be better. At least someone new won't be so corrupt and divisive. As long as Netanyahu's here, it's like a sword hanging over us."

After we drive away, it occurs to me that the first two decades of the twenty-first century have brought a lot of changes, and yet nothing is different. In 2001, after the failure of the Camp David Accords and the start of the Second Intifada, the Israeli left lost its unifying objective: peace with the Palestinians and with the Arab world. Since then, apart from the occasional blip, the left has been in constant decline. Israelis are drawn to right-wing or centrist parties and alliances like Blue and White (led by Benny Gantz, who presented himself as a viable rival to Netanyahu in the 2019 elections), which talk of stability and force and are helmed by army generals who tout their security credentials. These parties do not propose any great changes in Israelis' lives.

The left wing was not genuinely able to define its raison d'être after the collapse of the peace process in 2001. What, in fact, does it offer Israeli society? Left-wing parties have, at various times, campaigned on a social-democratic platform, principles of democracy and an independent justice system. But none of these appealed to the public. Israelis' suspicion of the left wing has not wavered.

The only thing that has been defining the Israeli left is its desire to unseat Bibi. There is no real political home for people who hold leftist views, perhaps because there are no ideas to define such a home. And so even if the wish to get rid of Netanyahu was shared by many Israelis, the vast majority of them remain on the right or at most in the centre. Jewish left-wing parties represent roughly 3 per cent of the electorate, and the alliance of Arab parties another 6 per cent, give or take. The Israeli left has been all but erased from the political map, despite the fact that tens of thousands of people are out on the streets protesting a right-wing leader.

Is the failure of Oslo and the costs it exacted the main reason? Or is it that left-wing parties were unable to articulate their aims and regain public trust in the wake of this failure? Perhaps it's the absence of charismatic leaders? Or could it be that the Israeli left cannot justify its existence as long as the Palestinian issue – namely, ending the occupation – is not at the heart of public discourse? The Israeli left has not found a way to define what it means to be on the left today, nor has it adequately responded to Israelis' fears or offered them hope untainted by risk.

*"We might already be living in a post-peace era"*

Israeli leftists have been galvanised by Netanyahu and his failed policies. But even if he were to vanish tomorrow, the political left wing would remain a marginal entity. This sounds almost inconceivable as we drive from Caesarea to Tel Aviv, past junctions full of protestors, black flags, crowds of people calling for change. This is exactly the moment when the opposition should be flourishing. But as results come in from the March election, the dire predictions are confirmed, with Meretz and Labor eking out 10 per cent of the vote between them – their best achievement in the past four elections. The Joint List, an alliance of Arab parties, splintered before the election and its constituents garner less than 9 per cent of the vote. For now, a true Jewish-Arab party, which I've been promoting for years and which, I believe, could bring about change (if not at the polls, then at least as a political home for many Israelis) is nowhere on the horizon. The Israeli political map comprises a right wing and a centre.

## Days of small things

In the peaceful days of the late '90s, the Oasis Casino in Jericho, built by the Palestinian Authority and foreign investors, became a prime entertainment destination. Busloads of Israelis arrived from all over the country every evening, and it was said to be one of the most profitable casinos in the world. For me and my friends, driving to Jericho at night was an adventure brought to us courtesy of the peace process. Gazing out at the black emptiness surrounding us, the occasional flash of light would appear from a shadowy hilltop. And at the end of the drive you'd be in a Palestinian-controlled city. But early in the Second Intifada, Palestinian militants began sheltering in the casino, and the Israeli army bombed it. It's been shut ever since. A Palestinian friend who recently saw the casino floor was surprised to find everything carefully preserved: poker and blackjack tables, chandeliers, cashier booths. A ghost-casino that could spring back to life at any moment.

I'm driving with the historian Avi Shilon, author of a biography of Menachem Begin, among other books. We met in the army, where we both had office jobs that involved trying to do as little as possible. It was just after Yitzhak Rabin's assassination, and we were struggling to come to terms with it.

As we near the outskirts of Jericho and spot the blurry lights of the city, I suggest we take a detour to see the casino.

"Forget it. Maybe another time," Avi says.

"Are you afraid?"

"Of course. I haven't been near this place for twenty years."

We think back to the time we were almost killed on this road. We were on our way to the casino when the driver of a car coming in the other direction lost control, flinging two other vehicles onto the shoulder, and crashed into us. A drunk kid driving without a licence. We both walked away in one piece, but it was our last trip to the casino.

"It seems funny now that we saw the casino as a symbol of peace," Avi reminisces. "We really didn't understand much."

"Do you think we're the last generation for whom this place has any meaning? Is the conflict with the Palestinians something that only preoccupies us and the older generation?"

"For us it was the main thing," Avi says, "but we might already be living in a post-peace era. There are no more terrorist attacks, no more bloody conflict. It's possible that even though there's no peace, Israelis accept this state as the best we can get. Peace used to be the central issue, but it didn't work when the peace camp pushed it."

I remark that in some ways we are traumatised, politically, because we experienced hope followed by disillusionment at a young age. "Is that why we still feel we have no political home?" I wonder aloud.

"We also experienced the assassination of Rabin. Think back to those days. That was the most difficult thing our generation lived through. You and I used to talk about the assassination for hours upon hours, night after night. It haunted us for years."

"How do you think it affected us?"

"I personally lost some of my faith in grand ideas, even in politics."

"But if that's our reason for being stuck, why hasn't the younger generation revitalised the left?"

"Because the right wing brought stability to the country," Avi explains simply. "The public has no reason to gamble on something else."

"Could it just be a question of leadership? Some people say that if Rabin hadn't been assassinated, things would have been different."

"I don't think Rabin would have made peace with the Palestinians. The differences were too great – we saw that at Camp David. But there's a sense among the left that we weren't given a fair chance to promote peace, because of Rabin's assassination. You could look at things differently, though. I believed in peace in the '90s like you did, but in retrospect maybe it's a good thing that our generation failed, because it doesn't seem to have been the right path. Peace will probably not be achieved on the basis of land, of borders drawn between us and the Palestinians. It will come from the people – a grassroots peace, with ending curbs on freedom of movement as its priority."

"Do you really believe that?"

"Sometimes. There's a beautiful phrase that's used in the Bible when the narrative skips thirty or forty years ahead – 'days of small things'. Meaning, nothing happening. Maybe Israelis looked at the '90s and concluded that we didn't need any grand initiatives. Ironically, for most of the years under right-wing governments, the 'days of small things' seemed to have worked."

"But now the stability Netanyahu boasted of is dead," I counter. "The country is in chaos because of the pandemic and its mishandling. Yet support for left-wing parties is still negligible. So what should the left have done after 2001, to avoid becoming irrelevant?"

"That's a difficult question," Avi concedes as we drive out of the desert and spot a glow on the horizon, which means we're getting close to Jerusalem. "The working class in Israel is very suspicious of the left. Most of them are Mizrahim, and they've viewed the right wing as their political voice for many years. That's also because they perceive the Labor Party as having marginalised them in the first decades of the state. The left lost the Haredim as partners, too. So when it comes to socio-economic issues, there isn't really anyone for the left to turn to. In the realm of the conflict with the Palestinians, the left has had no message since the Second Intifada. And other issues, like the environment or even ensuring greater democracy, are not important enough in a state that still votes on security concerns. The peace process was the concept that bolstered and defined the left. When it died, all the air was let out of the balloon. And they still haven't figured out how to re-inflate it."

## *In the Likud stronghold*

Like many towns in the south of Israel, Netivot is a Likud stronghold. Tel Avivians still recall the impoverished town from news reports in the '90s, but in the past decade there have been significant changes here. By many economic standards, Netivot is a success story.

The first place I visit is the local Likud headquarters. There are so many identical town squares here that I lose my way, but then I catch sight of some little Likud and Israeli flags, and balloons above a staircase. The handful of people sitting outside look tired: a few members of the Knesset paid a visit last night. I try not to step on the crumpled signs lying around.

There used to be tensions between the political camps in Netivot, but today those are distant memories. The activists here talk about Labor and the left wing with an ironic smile, sometimes sounding almost nostalgic.

I ask why they think right-wing parties are in power, and they talk about the Jewish state: the right is perceived as more Jewish than the left. They also credit Netivot's growth to Likud, which, they maintain, has brought economic progress to the Mizrahi population. They mention personal security, a topic that comes up in many meetings with right-wingers. Israelis are safer than they've ever been, they say. Some aren't pleased with how Likud is handling the pandemic, but they don't see how any other party could have done better.

A contractor named Hajabi takes me on a walking tour of one of the new neighbourhoods. The skyline is dotted with yellow cranes. We see several residential complexes surrounded by lawns, with new buildings in various stages of construction.

"Tell me, Baram," he says, "you're interested in the right wing, in Likud, but I want to ask you about the left. Sometimes I miss those days when there were lefties here. My grandchildren don't believe me when I tell them there was a big Labor Party office right here in Netivot. So where has the left disappeared to?"

I laugh. "That's what I keep asking myself. Do you know what I feel, more than anything else? The absence of a political home. New centre-left parties spring up and disappear and reform, but there's no home. I look at you and I think: here are people who have a political home."

"That's interesting," Hajabi observes. "I wasn't always pleased with Likud. There were times when I voted for them without a good enough reason ..."

"But you always voted Likud?"

"Yes. Always. That's the definition of a political home, isn't it? That even when times aren't so good, you stick with it."

## The right wing and power

Netanyahu, before he was replaced by his former ally Naftali Bennett, flaunted a few major accomplishments over his decade-long rule: security (there are no terrorist attacks), economic prosperity, stability and normalised relations with some Arab states, which have recently become public. In other words, no earthquakes. A large portion of Israeli society believes these claims and is willing to forgive him for the corruption he stands accused of. True, Netanyahu made no attempt to resolve the Israeli–Palestinian conflict or offer a future for the Gaza Strip, and there have been regular escalations leading to military operations – but most Israelis see this state of affairs as the best-case scenario. During the pandemic, however, two of Netanyahu's primary achievements fizzled. The economy suffered a catastrophic blow, with many Israelis losing their jobs, and the pandemic management was chaotic: decisions were reversed almost daily, people were not getting the help they desperately need, and millions of children were out of school for over a year. And then, in May 2021, another of his highly touted achievements – security – was shattered. Rockets were landing in Israel every night, Tel Aviv was under attack, Israelis were fearful and hopeless, the streets were as empty as they'd been in the Second Intifada, and after nearly two weeks of war it was hard to envision any genuine improvement. At the March election, Netanyahu's Likud had still emerged as the largest party in Israel, with around 60 per cent of the vote going to the right (depending

*It almost seemed as if they hadn't bothered to consider the conflict until the rockets hurled it back into their consciousness*

on how one classifies a right-wing party that wants to get rid of Netanyahu). The Israeli left had failed to persuade voters that it constitutes an alternative to Netanyahu, even at the height of a crisis. During the subsequent military escalation, the so-called leaders on the left displayed a dispiriting failure to offer anything new – no solutions, no plans, no vision. It almost seemed as if they hadn't bothered to consider the Israeli–Palestinian conflict until the rockets hurled it back into their consciousness. Even when Netanyahu's policy of ignoring the conflict became so manifestly untenable, the opposition could offer no alternative, having ignored – much as the right wing had – Israel's most pivotal problem for so many years.

During Netanyahu's lengthy reign, my son Daniel asked me a lot of questions about him. Of all the Israeli politicians, he's the only one whose name Daniel knows. He hears things at kindergarten and elsewhere, and he wanted to know how Netanyahu was able to be prime minister for so long. It's a good question. The striking protest movement that took place on the streets and outside the prime minister's residence was focused on Netanyahu's corruption, an issue that is not a priority for Israelis struggling to survive. None of the left-wing leaders seems able to reach Israelis who have valid fears for their future. Even if these leaders could offer solutions, it's quite possible that most Israelis wouldn't listen. Years of discussing nothing but Netanyahu's corruption have created this huge ideological vacuum in the progressive camp.

The peace process was killed by the illusion that every aspect of a century-long conflict could be solved at a single summit, rather than through a lengthy reconciliation process. The left seems to have adopted the view that if "total peace" is not attainable, there is little else to do. Whereas there are, in fact, steps that could and should be advocated by the left: equal rights for all residents of

Jerusalem, dismantling the smaller settlements that have been built only as a provocation, allowing Gazans to work in Israel, eliminating many of the checkpoints and negotiating a lasting ceasefire with Hamas. All these would contribute to a decrease in tensions, yet we have heard not even the vaguest such plans from the progressive camp.

It's hard to make sense of how the regime's opposition could grow weaker in the face of such colossal failures. Some on the left accuse Netanyahu himself, claiming that his incitement has delegitimised left-wing parties in the eyes of most Israelis. Even if this is true – and Netanyahu was, without a doubt, an inciting and divisive prime minister – one cannot lay all the blame on one's adversary, who is understandably determined to win. The Israeli left's inability to speak to broad sectors of the public and offer a vision of the future is a far more profound predicament. And the departure of Netanyahu will not save the camp that once hoped to shape the future of Israel and is now on life support. ▤

# The end of ideology?

## *Pragmatism in the Middle East*

## Lina Khatib

In 2017, on his first overseas trip as president, Donald Trump, accompanied by his wife Melania and son-in-law Jared Kushner, flew to Saudi Arabia to attend the Riyadh summit. Not surprisingly, he was lavishly received. He participated in a traditional *'ardah* sword dance and was photographed with King Salman and Egypt's president, Abdel-Fattah al-Sisi, their hands placed on a glowing orb.

In fact, three summits took place in Riyadh over two days during Trump's trip: a US–Saudi bilateral that included signing an arms deal worth US$350 billion, the largest in world history; the Gulf Cooperation Council; and the Organisation of Islamic Cooperation, which was boycotted by Iran and Turkey. On 21 May, Air Force One flew directly on to Israel – a historic journey which symbolised a desire for better relations between these two long-standing US allies in the Middle East.

Nearly four years later, Trump's Democratic successor, President Joe Biden, took several weeks to even initiate a telephone call to either King Salman or Benjamin Netanyahu, Israel's then prime minister. Biden had been sharply critical of the kingdom's role in the war in

Yemen and the brutal murder of the journalist Jamal Khashoggi in Istanbul, and was seen as hostile to Netanyahu's positions on peace with the Palestinians and Iran. When Biden finally travelled abroad – in June 2021 – he went to Europe, not the Middle East.

Biden's election victory had brought some cautious hope that the United States might pursue a more measured path towards the region. Yet he was expected to continue the gradual US disengagement from the Middle East that occurred during Trump's presidency and, before that, Barack Obama's eight years in the White House, when other regions, especially Asia, were considered more important.

Whether through engagement or disengagement, US foreign policy, especially regarding Iran, will continue to have a substantial impact on the Middle East's future. But the region's power balance is changing, becoming more complicated. The influence of other actors – mainly Russia, Turkey, Iran and Gulf Arab states, as well as China on the economic front – has grown, partly due to the disengagement by the previous two US administrations. And the tensions, conflicts and shifting rivalries and alliances of the Middle East can no longer be explained in terms of ideological or religious divides.

Countries cooperate on certain issues but disagree on others. Alliances develop, then shift. Political, economic and security goals are compartmentalised. The defining characteristic of Middle East geopolitics is pragmatism.

Traditional principles and allegiances are giving way to realpolitik.


### The Saudi–Iranian rivalry

The battle for influence between Saudi Arabia and Iran has developed into one of the oldest rivalries in the Middle East – and is a source of much of the region's political and military polarisation.

The rivalry began to brew during the days of rule of the Shah of Iran, as Saudi Arabia was concerned about the Shah's involvement in the Gulf – including his 1968 declaration of Bahrain as Iranian territory, the 1971 seizure of three islands claimed by the UAE, and the continuation of selling oil to the West and Israel in 1967 and 1973, in defiance of the Arab oil embargoes. But it was the creation of the Islamic Republic of Iran, with its expansionist ideology and its aim of "exporting the Islamic revolution" to the Middle East and beyond, that became a direct challenge to Saudi Arabia's influence, both abroad and domestically. Iran wanted to court the Shia citizens of other countries in the Middle East, like Lebanon and Iraq, as well as the 10–15 per cent of Saudi nationals who are Shia.

But the Saudi–Iranian rivalry is often reduced – wrongly – to ideological differences and sectarian tensions between Sunni and Shia Islam. The two Islamic sects were indeed born of disagreements over the political and religious leadership of Muslims following the death of the Prophet Mohammed, but this evolved over centuries to be more about power than religion. Historically, political leaders from each sect sought to exert power over their opponents, but neither side succeeded in overwhelming the other. The creation of the Islamic Republic of Iran was the first and only time a Shia state came to exist in modern times, which posed a threat to Sunni-majority Saudi Arabia. But the rivalry between the two countries is driven by their desires to consolidate a position of political – rather than ideological – leadership in the Middle East. For both, ideology is a tool for obtaining power and influence.

Iran's strategy for exporting the revolution relied to a large extent on soft power, for example aid and religious outreach. Over the years, it sponsored organisations offering services such as medical provision and education to underprivileged Shia communities across the Arab world, and trained Shia clerics who would spend time in Iran's religious schools and then go back to their countries of origin to preach and rally support for the Supreme Leader (first Ayatollah Khomeini and then his successor, Khamenei).

Saudi Arabia began to see this outreach as a threat, and accelerated its own ideological export project – spreading ultraconservative Sunni Wahhabism in the Middle East and beyond. Under King Faisal in the 1960s and 1970s, Saudi Arabia had used soft power abroad, such as sponsoring training for Sunni clerics who followed the Wahhabi doctrine. The Islamic revolution in Iran, along with the takeover of the Grand Mosque in Saudi Arabia later that year by Saudi extremists calling for the overthrow of the House of Saud, pushed then-ruler King Khaled to make Wahhabism dominant inside Saudi Arabia. This brought a rising conservatism that led to the closing of cinemas in the early 1980s, the upholding of a ban on women from driving that had been in place since 1957, and other strict social measures. To bolster the House of Saud's religious legitimacy, in the 1980s the king of Saudi Arabia resurrected the title of Custodian of the Two Holy Mosques (*khadem al-haramein*), and began using it instead of 'His Majesty'.

> *Saudi Arabia's focus has shrunk to domestic and Gulf-region issues rather than broader Arab ones*

For decades, the race between Iran's Shia regional project and Saudi Arabia's Sunni Wahhabi project dominated political and religious discourse on the Middle East. Countries such as Lebanon came to be seen as playgrounds for Saudi–Iranian rivalry, especially as Iran's involvement in Arab countries went beyond social outreach. Iran has sponsored myriad armed groups in the Middle East, including Hezbollah in Lebanon (since the 1980s), the Houthis in Yemen (since the 2010s) and the Popular Mobilization Units (PMUs) in Iraq (since 2014). In Lebanon and Iraq, Hezbollah and the PMUs have respectively become the most powerful political and military actors, consolidating Iran's regional influence: Hezbollah and its allies claimed most parliamentary seats in Lebanon in the last election, and the PMUs have formed political parties that also won significant seats in the Iraqi parliamentary elections, in addition to dominating Iraq's security apparatus and state institutions. Both have been involved in fighting in the war in Syria to support the regime of Bashar al-Assad, which is not a Shia regime but is a political ally of Iran's.

Although Saudi Arabia also sponsored extremist armed Sunni groups around the world, including factions of the Muslim Brotherhood till 1990 and Jaysh al-Fatah in Syria in the mid-2010s, it is Iran's proxies that are dominant today. In Lebanon, Iraq and Yemen, political and/or military rivals to Iran's proxies proved to be weak and did not benefit from the same level of Saudi or Western support. In 2014, Saudi Arabia designated the Muslim Brotherhood as a terrorist organisation and focused its support on non-extremist political and military Syrian groups opposed to the Assad regime. The halting of Saudi support pushed Jaysh al-Fatah to cease to exist in 2017. Since 2017, Saudi Arabia itself has shifted its strategy with the rise of Crown Prince Mohammed bin Salman, known as MBS. Bin Salman has been trying to transform Saudi society so that it becomes more open, to diversify the economy beyond its longstanding reliance on oil, and to make Saudi Arabia attractive to foreign investors. To achieve that, he has recognised that it is necessary to curtail the influence of Wahhabi clerics and significantly lessen the kingdom's support of armed Islamist groups.

Saudi Arabia's focus has consequently shrunk to domestic and Gulf-region issues rather than broader Arab ones. Its influence in Lebanon and Iraq has become minimal, and it is no longer trying to topple the Iranian-backed regime of Bashar al-Assad in Syria. That is largely because of Russia's military intervention to support the Damascus regime and the United States' disengagement, both of which paved the way for Iran's influence in Syria to grow – especially after the United States signed the nuclear deal with Iran in 2015. The reduction of Saudi interventions in the Middle East has indeed allowed Iran to consolidate its influence through its proxies in Lebanon, Yemen, Iraq and Syria. This consolidation, however, has cost Iran wider popular support among those Sunnis who had previously seen Iran's proxies such as Hezbollah as an important force of resistance against Israel.

Saudi Arabia's support for Sunni politicians in Lebanon has also dwindled. It no longer sees investing in its local allies as a necessity since these allies, like former prime minister Saad Hariri, have been – in Saudi Arabia's eyes – too weak to stand up to Hezbollah. In Iraq, Saudi Arabia maintains good relations with the current president and the prime minister, but these political leaders are not able to suppress their armed pro-Iranian rivals, especially the PMUs. In Syria, Russia's military intervention in 2015 was the main reason behind Saudi Arabia's failure in its attempts to remove the Assad regime. The Russian intervention and Moscow's pragmatic alliance with Iran in support of the Assad regime presented Iran and its proxy groups like Hezbollah with another opportunity to score points against Saudi Arabia.

Bin Salman, who was the minister of defence before his father appointed him crown prince, has been spearheading a military campaign in Saudi Arabia's next-door neighbour Yemen, targeting the Iran-backed Houthis there. But the campaign has not yet succeeded. The Houthis have been stubbornly rejecting political compromises proposed by Riyadh, feeling empowered because the might of the Saudi-led, US-supported military campaign against them  has not been enough to deliver a much-needed, face-saving victory.

All this underlines the fact that Iran's influence in the Middle East – extending from Yemen through Iraq and into the Levant – is greater than ever, while Saudi Arabia's influence has reduced. And it shows that both actors have been motivated by pragmatism rather than ideology in their approach to gaining influence in the Arab world.


## *Biden and Iran*

Iran's growing profile as a regional actor in the Middle East has been met with alarm by both Saudi Arabia and Israel. It also worried Trump, who considered Obama to be too lenient towards Tehran.

Believing that Iran's nuclear enrichment program posed the greatest threat to regional security, the Obama administration pursued a nuclear deal with Tehran. Negotiations focused exclusively on enrichment, ignoring other activities like Iran's ballistic missile program and interventions in Arab countries like Iraq and Syria. Obama was careful not to link the Syria crisis with the nuclear file, prioritising a deal with Iran before the end of his presidency. This stance was a cause of concern for Saudi Arabia and Israel, which both worked behind the scenes – unsuccessfully – to prevent an agreement. In Vienna in July 2015, Iran and the United States, along with five other nations and the European Union, reached a deal, known as the Joint Comprehensive Plan of Action.

In contrast, Trump withdrew from the JCPOA in May 2018 and instead pursued what became known as a "maximum pressure" strategy. He ramped up sanctions on Iran and cajoled US allies to follow suit – or at least not to cross the lines laid down by the US sanctions. Washington believed economic pressure would push Tehran to modify its behaviour and accept political compromises. However, the Iranian regime proved to be highly resilient. It was able, for example, to use Iraq as an economic go-between to circumvent sanctions.

Despite Trump's hard-line stance, Iran's influence in neighbouring Iraq grew significantly during his term. Iran viewed the rise of the Islamic State terrorist organisation as a threat and deployed Iranian and Iraqi militias to fight against it, thereby increasing its footprint in Iraq. In addition, the United States' mishandling of the domestic situation in Iraq in the aftermath of the US-led invasion in 2003 paved the way for corruption and poor governance to permeate national institutions, and allowed Shia and non-Shia actors alike to increase their power and wealth at the expense of the Iraqi state. Iraq has a Shia majority population, many of whom support the Iranian regime. Iran's influence in Syria, Lebanon and Yemen also reached unprecedented heights.

Under the Biden administration, though, US pressure is taking a different form: it is based on offering Iran incentives to change its behaviour. Biden has taken steps to re-enter the nuclear deal, but is not simply resurrecting Obama-era policy. He is also seeking to negotiate with Iran over the latter's regional involvement, though apparently only after the United States re-joins the JCPOA. Saudi Arabia has expressed caution about this approach, worrying that offers to lift sanctions in return for the US re-joining the JCPOA could present a clear win for Tehran. But Riyadh has welcomed US negotiations over the JCPOA as a step towards addressing Iran's regional interventions, reacting positively to US signals about the desire to end the Yemen conflict. For Iran, it would be much easier to compromise on Yemen than on Iraq, Syria and Lebanon, which are more strategically important because of their geographical proximity and the influence of its key proxies there. Saudi Arabia may well accept a scenario in which the United States re-joins the JCPOA while Iran significantly rolls back its activities in Yemen but retains some influence in the Levant. For the Biden administration, succeeding in the nuclear negotiations and ending the war in Yemen would also be a useful step in demonstrating US leadership in other international conflicts in the Middle East, potentially paving the way for greater involvement in resolving the ongoing crises in Syria or Libya.

Iran's expanding activities in the Middle East have made it a major destabilising force in the region. The nuclear agreement did not encourage the country to curb its regional involvement – if anything, its interventions increased after the signing of the JCPOA, while Saudi Arabia's influence weakened. Syria has paid the greatest price for the nuclear deal. Its fate was effectively sacrificed for the sake of a deal that was never comprehensive enough to limit Iran's destabilising actions. It remains to be seen whether the Biden administration's carrot-and-stick approach towards Iran (restoring the nuclear deal while also addressing Iran's regional activities) will succeed in pushing Tehran to modify its behaviour.

### *Turkey and Russia advance*

US disengagement from the Middle East during the Obama and Trump administrations paved the way for other actors to increase their influence, especially Turkey and Russia. Under Obama, Washington often rhetorically supported movements calling for freedom and democracy in the Middle East but did little to transform words into action. During his two terms, democratic movements in the region as well as allied autocratic regimes felt let down by US policy. Trump generally neither spoke nor acted in support of such movements. Instead, on more than one occasion he abruptly announced his intention to withdraw US troops from the Middle East, only for decisions to be rolled back shortly after. In the Trump era, resentment towards US foreign policy by Arab democratic movements continued, but Saudi Arabia felt better supported due to the tougher approach towards Iran.

*US disengagement from Syria weakened its own ally and empowered an American rival*

Turkey intervened quite heavily in the Syrian conflict. Initially, President Erdoğan threw his weight behind factions of the Syrian opposition that were seeking the removal of Assad. But his main aim has been to prevent an autonomous Kurdish region from being established near Turkey's border by Syrian Kurds linked to the Kurdistan Workers' Party (or PKK), a paramilitary group Turkey and the United States both consider a terrorist organisation. When, in the fight against ISIS, the United States and its allies began a pragmatic partnership with PKK-affiliated Kurdish forces to establish the Syrian Democratic Forces, Turkey increased its intervention by occupying Syrian territory in the north of the country.

Turkey again intervened militarily in Libya to support the UN-recognised Libyan government in Tripoli against eastern Libyan forces led by General Khalifa Haftar, who was in turn supported by the UAE and Egypt – both hostile to Erdoğan. Turkey also arranged the transfer of Syrian mercenaries into Libya to aid its military campaign there. Its main aims in Libya are to secure a role for itself in the wake of the discovery of gas in the Eastern Mediterranean (especially as Turkey has been excluded from the East Mediterranean Gas Forum); gain access to military bases; and increase political influence over the Tripoli government.

Russia aspires to the same goals as Turkey in Libya, making the two countries rivals. Moscow and Ankara have also faced off in Syria. Russia found in that conflict an opportunity to assert itself vis-à-vis the West, and the United States in particular. Vladimir Putin began his military intervention in Syria in 2015 in support of Assad, entering a pragmatic alliance with Iran that saw the Russian air force complementing the Tehran-backed militias on the ground. Russia's presence in Syria became a challenge for Turkey, but Putin later involved Turkey and Iran in the Astana Process to try to reach a ceasefire, presenting Russia as the kingmaker among the three. Russia then began reaching out to the US-backed Syrian Democratic Forces in the north-east, setting up joint military posts to monitor Turkish-governed areas in Syria.

Russia's military approach to Syria and Libya therefore reflects pragmatism – and pursuit of geopolitical prominence – rather than ideological or long-term strategic alignments. The absence of an active diplomatic role for the United States in the Syrian and Libyan conflicts has facilitated the rise of Turkey and Russia's influence in the Middle East and North Africa. Russia's military intervention in Syria also killed off Saudi Arabia's attempt to unify the Syrian opposition under one political umbrella. In this way, US disengagement from Syria weakened its own ally and empowered an American rival.

## The Gulf divides

With both regional and foreign actors vying for influence, the Middle East's current geopolitical camps are fluid. Countries may cooperate on certain issues but compete on others. And alliances that once appeared to be enduring have crumbled. Nowhere is this more apparent than in the relationships between Arab monarchies.

The Gulf Cooperation Council – a six-nation grouping based in Riyadh – was once regarded as a stable alliance. But, in recent years, the UAE, Bahrain and Saudi Arabia – as well as Egypt, which is not a council member – have become increasingly frustrated with Qatar's geopolitical ambitions. Qatar has moved from being a small, wealthy country with a large public-relations footprint (due to its investment in media outlets like *Al-Jazeera*) to a regional competitor with Saudi Arabia. For example, Saudi Arabia and Qatar largely supported different factions of the Syrian opposition from 2012 to 2015. Pro-Qatari and pro-Saudi Syrian factions did not trust one another and refused to coordinate their military actions against the Assad regime. This division played into the hands of Iran, Russia and Assad, and contributed to the weakening of opposition institutions like the Syrian National Council, which at one point featured a president considered loyal to Saudi Arabia and a deputy president from the pro-Qatar camp. In 2017 Saudi Arabia – joined by the UAE, Bahrain and Egypt – spearheaded a boycott campaign against Qatar, suspending flights to Doha, blockading ships and trying to isolate Qatar economically and politically by severing diplomatic ties. The United States has chosen not to take sides in the Gulf crisis.

The fragmentation over Qatar was reflected in the war in Yemen. In 2011, Saudi Arabia halted the popular movement calling for regime change in Sana'a that arose as part of the Arab Spring protests. Through the Gulf Initiative, Riyadh arranged the handing over of power from Yemeni president Ali Abdullah Saleh to his deputy – a pro-Saudi figure – angering Yemeni activists who had hoped for regime change, as well as Qatar, which had hoped Saleh would be replaced with a pro-Qatari figure. As in Syria, divisions on Yemen among Gulf countries benefited Iran, which looked to widen its influence further by supporting the Houthi rebels, who tried to take over the country and sparked a bloody civil war.

In 2015, Saudi Arabia decided to launch a military campaign against the Houthis, with support from the UAE and the United States. In 2019, however, concerned about being a target for Iranian retaliation, Abu Dhabi decided to withdraw from the campaign. Since then, the UAE has embarked on an ambitious plan to increase its own influence in the Middle East. Unlike Qatar, it has avoided antagonising Saudi Arabia, helped by the close relationship between the UAE leader, Mohamed bin Zayed, and Saudi crown prince MBS. The Biden administration continues to support Riyadh in Yemen but, in an attempt at encouraging a peace deal and maintaining humanitarian aid to Yemen, has cancelled the designation of the Houthis as a terrorist group, much to Saudi Arabia's disappointment.

Saudi Arabia and the UAE have both been acting pragmatically in their pursuit of geopolitical influence. Aside from MBS's process of liberalisation, Riyadh has reached out to the leadership in Iraq so that the kingdom retains some influence within its neighbour at a time when Tehran's sway over Baghdad has grown. Seeking a way out of the Yemen conflict, Saudi Arabia has participated in a number of talks with Tehran in Baghdad, though Iraq does not have the leverage over either actor to push for a conflict resolution. Saudi Arabia, alongside Egypt, has also been courted by Turkey, which does not want to remain isolated in the Eastern Mediterranean.

Russia, for its part, is trying to capitalise on Saudi weariness about both the Biden administration's objective of re-joining the nuclear deal with Iran and its change of designation of the Houthis. In April 2021, Russian foreign minister Sergei Lavrov visited Riyadh and Abu Dhabi and announced that Russia would coordinate with Qatar and Turkey regarding the Syrian conflict. Strengthening Saudi–Russian relations would support Moscow's goals of increasing its influence in the Middle East. Lavrov's visit again illustrated Putin's ambition to be seen as a key powerbroker in the Syrian crisis. However, disagreements between Saudi Arabia and Russia over the pace of oil supply increases (when the Covid-19 pandemic led to a drop in global demand) are a reminder that Saudi–Russian cooperation is not a step towards the formation of a broader alliance. Russia is not likely to replace the US as a strategic partner for Saudi Arabia.

> *The UAE has risen from a country widely seen as an economic hub to a regional power in the making*

The UAE, meanwhile, has been pursuing a bolder path. With Iran posing a continuous risk to its security, the Emiratis decided to opt for deterrence rather than confrontation. Supported by the United States during the latter months of the Trump administration, the UAE announced the brokering of a normalisation deal with Israel known as the Abraham Accords in August 2020. The Accords allow the two countries (plus Bahrain) to cooperate on economics and security. Emirati intelligence-sharing, security coordination and military cooperation with Israel bolster the UAE's standing in the face of Iranian activity in the Gulf. The Accords also increase the UAE's profile as an American ally and pave the way for it to play the role of regional powerbroker. Separately, the UAE and Israel have both strengthened their economic cooperation with China, despite American reservations about China's expanding global influence. The UAE has, for example, been manufacturing the Chinese Sinopharm Covid-19 vaccine and marketing it under the Arabic name Hayat (Life), while Israel has partnered with China to develop the port of Haifa.

The UAE has risen over the past few years from a country widely seen as an economic hub to a regional power in the making. Its pragmatic cooperation with the US, Israel and China, as well as its military involvement in Libya, indicate that it is pursuing its own path and no longer completely following the direction set by Saudi Arabia. Even when Abu Dhabi and Riyadh announced in March 2021 their willingness to re-engage with Doha, the UAE's relationship with Qatar remained much more lukewarm than Saudi Arabia's.

Saudi Arabia and the UAE remain allies with shared interests, but their pursuit of different paths shows that the Gulf region monarchies should not simply be viewed as one bloc. These two powerful Gulf nations are adept at compartmentalising their rivalries and partnerships. Both see the US as an essential ally, but the relative regional power of each of these monarchies will depend on American strategy on Iran.

## *Pragmatism and fragmentation*

The Middle East has long been seen as a region in which ideology ranks as a high priority, but its politics are now, more than ever, being driven by pragmatism. Some alliances are being created (like that between the UAE and Israel), while others unravel (like the UAE and Qatar). A region once seen as predictable is full of twists and turns.

A traditional power like Saudi Arabia is not only finding itself struggling to contain Iran but also witnessing the rise of the neighbouring UAE, which now has geopolitical ambitions of its own. An outside power like Russia has found in American disengagement an opportunity to present itself as a superpower once more. A regional power like Iran is at the peak of its influence in the Middle East but its position is precarious. A superpower like the United States is no longer engaging in the region with the intensity of the past.

Some external observers see US disengagement as having been an incentive for regional actors to try to solve their own problems, citing Iraq's mediation between Saudi Arabia and Iran, Turkey's efforts at rapprochement with Saudi Arabia and Egypt, and Russia's outreach to Gulf countries as examples. However, none of these developments marks a complete shift. Iraq's primary motivation for playing the role of Saudi–Iranian mediator is its geographical position between the two states, the place where some of their interests clash. Russia's outreach aims to add as many Middle Eastern and North African countries to its list of places that could, in its view, normalise relations with the Assad regime, which would enable reconstruction funds to flow into Syria and therefore international economic deals brokered by Russia. Turkey's warming of relations with Saudi Arabia and Egypt is happening at a time of heightened tension between Ankara and Tehran. US disengagement may have encouraged pragmatic behaviour by regional actors, but it has also led to increased fragmentation as each of them pursues individual interests rather than lasting alliances.

This complicated picture shows that the US remains essential to the region's future: both action and inaction have important consequences. Its approach towards Tehran's regional interventions is crucial, and will have a domino effect on all the other players. Some, like the UAE, pursue pragmatism to try to protect themselves regardless of what the US chooses to do on Iran. But others (like Saudi Arabia and Israel) clearly favour the development of a comprehensive US strategy on Iran that goes beyond the nuclear deal. The United States initiating negotiations over Iran's regional role alongside their nuclear negotiations would therefore have a placating effect on the region. Iran is not likely to respond to such negotiations by flexing its military muscles. If anything, the war between Israel and Hamas that flared up in May 2021 shows how Iranian-backed groups may feel empowered when the US ignores its role. Any moves by Washington to pull back from addressing Iran's regional intervention will only heighten regional rivalries and divergences. ▤

# Secret histories

## *Israel's road to normalisation*

## Elie Podeh

In March 2018, Israeli prime minister Benjamin Netanyahu visited Washington, DC, to deliver a speech at the annual conference of pro-Israel lobby group AIPAC (the American Israel Public Affairs Committee). While in the city he went out for dinner with his wife, Sara, at Café Milano, a Georgetown restaurant well-known as a dining spot for top administration officials. Coincidentally, the ambassador of the United Arab Emirates, Yousef al-Otaiba, was also dining there that night, with the Bahraini ambassador and a few senior Trump administration officials. Having served in Washington since 2008, Otaiba had developed close relations with many officials, including the Israeli ambassador Ron Dermer (2013–21). According to the then *New York Times* White House correspondent Mark Landler, one of Otaiba's dinner guests made contact with Netanyahu, who probably thought it was an opportunity that should not be missed. He and Sara went over to Otaiba's table. A short chat ensued, during which Netanyahu emphasised that Israel and the UAE had reasons to strengthen their relations against their mutual Iranian enemy.

In June 2020, when the idea of annexing part of the West Bank was floating in Israeli political circles following Trump's "deal of the century", Otaiba published an article in the popular Israeli daily *Yedioth Ahronoth*. Titled "Annexation or Normalisation", the article noted that many Arabs "would like to believe Israel is an opportunity, not an enemy. We face too many common dangers and see the great potential of warmer ties." Seeing this as a hint, the Trump administration seized the moment. On 13 August 2020, the US president made a dramatic announcement about the establishment of diplomatic relations between Israel and the UAE. Less than a month later, Bahrain followed suit. To consolidate and publicise the achievements, Trump convened a quadripartite summit in Washington on 15 September, where the United States, the UAE, Bahrain and Israel celebrated the signing of the Abraham Accords – a symbolic title which added a religious dimension to the agreements.

Normalisation continued with the announcement of a similar deal between Israel and Sudan, following a phone call between Trump, Netanyahu and the leaders of the Sudanese Interim Council, Abdel Fattah al-Burhan and Abdallah Hamdok, on 23 October. Morocco established relations with Israel on 10 December.

These agreements meant Israel had relations, public or secret, with thirteen out of twenty-two members of the Arab League. The four new partnerships prompted Trump, days before he left office in January 2021, to transfer Israel from the responsibility of the US European Command to the US Central Command (CENTCOM), which oversees the territory of the Middle East. CENTCOM has twenty members, including Egypt, Jordan and the Gulf states. This administrative decision was the culmination of a long process of Israel becoming a recognised – and desired – partner in the Middle

East by major Arab players and the West in the war against mutual enemies, such as Iran.

The process of Israel's integration into the Middle East has not yet been completed; some Arab and Muslim countries are still unwilling to recognise Israel or to deal openly with it. Many Arab people continue to object to Israel's existence, opposing peace while the Palestinian conflict remains unresolved. And resolution looked even more difficult to achieve after the East Jerusalem confrontations in May 2021 and the eruption of serious hostilities between Israel and Hamas in the Gaza Strip. However, the normalisation era does mark a significant change in Israel's position in the Middle East – and the roots of this era can be traced back to the early days following the country's establishment in 1948.

## *In the beginning*

In contrast to conventional wisdom, Israel was never completely isolated and ostracised in the region. In the post-1948 period, most Arab states were formally at war with Israel and boycotted it economically, but Israeli decision-makers still managed to find allies willing to cooperate secretly against common enemies. In the 1950s and 1960s, the West, Israel and pro-Western Middle East leaders shared an adversary – the Egyptian leader Gamal Abdel Nasser, who, with his pan-Arab ideology and support from the Soviet Union, sought to unify the Arab world. In its search for common allies against the Nasserist threat, Israel found Turkey and Iran, as well as Christian Ethiopia. Israel established what became known as the Alliance of the Periphery, which operated covertly until the fall of the Shah in the Islamic revolution of 1979. The most important mechanism of this triangle was the establishment of an intelligence apparatus called Trident, which enabled sharing of information between Israel, Turkey and Iran on mutual threats, particularly Nasserism and Communism. Though the pact was far from a fully-fledged alliance, it was still a genuine axis based on the need to cooperate against a common foe.

Israel also forged clandestine but intimate relations with Jordan's King Abdullah I until 1951, and with his grandson, King Hussein, from 1963 onwards. Though Jordan took part in the Six-Day War in 1967 (which led to the loss of the West Bank – known to Israelis as Judea and Samaria), the Hashemite Kingdom was considered Israel's "best of enemies". Israel and Jordan were friends in need and therefore friends indeed. Israel rescued Hussein during "Black September" in 1970, when the Palestine Liberation Organization (PLO), backed by Syria, tried to overthrow the king and establish a Palestinian state. Israel and Jordan, along with the West, shared a struggle against common threats, such as Palestinian guerrilla organisations and Islamic terrorism.

Other Arab monarchies secretly cooperated with Israel too. Morocco, under King Hassan II, established clandestine links with Israel in 1963, managed by the Mossad intelligence agency. Israel helped Morocco establish its secret service and even played a minor role in the assassination of opposition leader Mehdi Ben-Barka in France in 1965. In the 1970s and 1980s, Israel advised Rabat on the 2700-kilometre-long sand wall built between Morocco and Western Sahara, whose independence was sought by the Polisario movement with Algerian support. Israel also received access to the protocols of Arab League summits held in Morocco in 1965, 1981 and 1982.

In addition, Israel enjoyed access to the Gulf state of Oman starting in the early 1970s, helping Sultan Qaboos in his struggle against a rebellion supported by pro-communist elements in South

Yemen. Israel and Oman remained in secret contact until the formal establishment of diplomatic relations in 1996.

Forming secret links with minorities within otherwise hostile states was another method Israel employed, including with Christian Maronites in Lebanon, Christians in South Sudan and Muslim Kurds in Iraq. Some of Israel's decision-makers entertained the idea of building a "minorities alliance" that would unite several communities in the Middle East against the majority Muslim Arabs. Relations with the Maronites had existed since the 1940s, and Israel assisted certain factions in the 1958 and 1975–76 Lebanese civil wars. This set the stage for cooperation between Israel and the Phalange in the 1982 invasion of Lebanon, which ended in a fiasco: the Phalange betrayed Israeli expectations, and their leader – Bashir Gemayel – was assassinated by the Syrians

> *Partnership with Israel, even if secret, could serve as a deterrent against the mutual enemy*

after his election to the Lebanese presidency. Eighteen years later, in May 2000, Israel finally withdrew from Lebanon. Israel aided the Kurds in their struggle for independence from 1963 to 1975. This help was offered partly for moral reasons, and partly to strengthen Kurdish capacity to engage the Iraqi army, thereby reducing the threat of an attack on Israel's eastern front. And, finally, Israel helped the Christians in southern Sudan in their fight for autonomy against the predominantly Muslim regime in Khartoum. Israeli cooperation with the South Sudanese started in 1969 and continued intermittently until South Sudan's independence in 2011.

Each state or minority had its own reasons to cooperate with Israel, but all shared the need to forge allies against common enemies – in line with the well-known Arabic proverb "The enemy of my enemy is my friend" (*'adu 'aduwi sadiqi*). Middle Eastern countries and minorities also wanted to benefit from Israel's growing military power, particularly in the post-1967 period. Partnership with Israel, even if secret, could serve as a deterrent against the mutual enemy. Israel was in a position to provide arms and ammunition, whether Soviet-made and captured during the wars against Arab states, or domestically manufactured. A further motivation was to acquire support in civilian fields, such as agriculture, medicine, industry, desalination, cyber and other advanced technology. And, finally, Israel's image as an all-powerful force in Washington, DC, (even if exaggerated) was a recurrent reason for seeking its cooperation. Over the years, Israel has helped Egypt, Jordan, the UAE, Morocco and the Kurds to secure US approval for the purchase of arms and the granting of loans and financial support.

Likewise, Israel had its own reasons to cooperate with states and minorities in the region. It, too, had an interest in allying with "the enemy of my enemy". It wanted to extricate itself from self-perceived regional isolation and ostracism. In the absence of formal and public recognition of Israel, any cooperation – even if secret – bolstered the confidence of the country's decision-making elite. In the first decades after 1948, Israel wanted to convince the US that it was a regional power to be reckoned with, leading successive administrations to guarantee its survival. This insecurity on the part of Israeli governments was born of the historical Jewish experience of persecution, of which the Shoah was the most dramatic manifestation. Finally, Israel shared a sense of solidarity with some communities across the Middle East, particularly the Kurds in Iraq and the Maronites in Lebanon, who were similarly surrounded by a powerful and hostile majority.

## *"Flirtations" with Israel*

The first major change in Arab attitudes to Israel occurred after the Six-Day War. There was a growing realisation that Israel was a fait accompli; that their own domestic concerns were far more important than the Palestinian issue; and that they shared interests and enemies with Israel. A second, more important, change occurred in the wake of the Oslo Accords with the Palestinians in 1993. Five Arab states – Oman, Qatar, Tunisia, Morocco and Mauritania – opened diplomatic missions in Israel in the second half of the 1990s and abrogated the Arab boycott, following Egypt and Jordan. Other Arab countries – Bahrain, the UAE and Saudi Arabia – began maintaining secret relations with Israel from the mid-1990s. Though some of these ties were severed due to the Second Intifada (2000–04), the second Lebanese war between Israel and Hezbollah in 2006 consolidated cooperation between Israel and Arab countries against Iran, albeit covertly. The Islamic republic was determined to develop nuclear capabilities in order to achieve a dominant, if not hegemonic, position in the Middle East, through alliances with political and ideological proxies (such as Syria, Hezbollah, Shiite elements in Iraq and the Houthis in Yemen). In addition, the Gulf states of Saudi Arabia, the UAE and Bahrain found an interest in cooperating against Sunni jihadist elements, such as al-Qaeda and the Islamic State (ISIS), as well as Hamas and Islamic Jihad in Gaza, which are indirectly supported by Turkey, Qatar and Iran.

Saudi Arabia's "flirtation" with Israel goes back to two peace initiatives. The first, proposed in 1981 by Crown Prince Fahd, offered a vague recognition of Israel in return for full Israeli withdrawal to the 1967 boundaries, and the establishment of an independent Palestinian state with Jerusalem as its capital. This unsatisfactory initiative was flatly rejected by Israel. The second Saudi initiative was launched in 2002, by Crown Prince Abdallah. A modified version was adopted by an Arab League summit in Beirut and termed the Arab Peace Initiative (API). It offered the establishment of full relations with the twenty-two members of the Arab League in return for Israeli withdrawal from the territories occupied in 1967 and the establishment of a Palestinian state in the West Bank and Gaza, with East Jerusalem as its capital. The 2002 initiative was also accepted by the fifty-seven-member Organisation of Islamic Cooperation, including Iran. Regrettably, Israel has never officially responded to the API.

Israel's war against Hezbollah in 2006 reflected a broader conflict between the pro-Iranian axis on one side and Israel and the moderate Arab camp on the other. This paved the way for a historic meeting in Amman in September that year between Israeli prime minister Ehud Olmert, accompanied by Mossad chief Meir Dagan, and Prince Bandar bin Sultan, the head of the Saudi National Security Council. Bandar had a long history of meetings with Israelis and American Jewish leaders when serving as ambassador in Washington, DC. In 2010, Dagan secretly flew to Saudi Arabia to meet his intelligence counterparts. The cooperation culminated eventually in another secret meeting (leaked by the Israeli side) between Prime Minister Benjamin Netanyahu, the US secretary of state Mike Pompeo and Saudi crown prince Mohammed bin Salman (MBS) in the Saudi Arabian city of Neom in November 2020. MBS represents the new generation of Saudi leaders which, in contrast to the older generation represented by his father, King Salman, is willing to strengthen links with Israel regardless of the Palestinian problem. His image in the United States and the West, however, has been tainted by his involvement in the assassination of dissident journalist Jamal Khashoggi at the Saudi consulate in Istanbul in 2018.

Israel's relations with the UAE began in the aftermath of the Oslo agreements, when the UAE gained Israeli prime minister Rabin's consent to the sale of F-16 fighters by the US – a move reminiscent of the Abraham Accords, when Israel agreed to the sale of F-35s. The major change occurred following the 2004 death of UAE federation president Sheikh Zayed bin Sultan Al Nahyan and the rise of a younger, more daring and pro-Western generation, especially of Crown Prince Mohammed binZayed Al Nahyan (MBZ). Since then, and as fear of the Iranian threat grew, secret Israeli–UAE relations in the security and economic spheres proliferated. Israel's 2010 Dubai hotel assassination of Mahmoud al-Mabhouh, a Hamas operative responsible for smuggling weapons from Iran to Gaza, temporarily soured relations but US mediation led the two to renew their clandestine cooperation. And Israel scored a major diplomatic achievement in 2015 when the UAE agreed to Israeli representation at the Abu Dhabi-based UN International Renewable Energy Agency (IRENA) established in 2009. Thus, both the Mossad and the Israeli foreign ministry maintained secret relations on a regular basis with the UAE. In addition, Otaiba, the UAE ambassador in Washington, kept open channels with the Israeli ambassador and many American Jewish leaders. His meeting with Netanyahu at Café Milano, though surprising, was in line with his ongoing secret activity vis-à-vis Israel.

Simultaneously, Bahrain developed secret ties with the Mossad from the mid-2000s. In addition, in 2009, the Israeli foreign ministry established clandestine links in the capital, Manama, under the cover of a foreign company. This, along with secret meetings between Israeli and Bahraini foreign ministers, laid the grounds for the ultimate deal – the signing of the Abraham Accords between Israel, the UAE and Bahrain. It was the public manifestation of a process which existed for at least two decades behind the scenes.

## The ultimate deal

Until recently, the conventional assumption was that Arab states would not normalise relations with Israel before a resolution of the Palestinian problem. So what has changed?  First, the Trump administration was willing to pay generously for Arab normalisation with Israel, and various states were keen to take advantage of this narrow window of opportunity. The UAE received an unprecedented arms deal, including the world's most advanced fighter jets; Sudan was removed from the list of terror-supporting states, which is worth a fortune in Western loans and investments; and Morocco's annexation of the internationally disputed Western Sahara was recognised by the United States. In addition, Arab states were concerned that the new Biden administration would renew the 2015 nuclear agreement with Iran, which Trump had abandoned. A public alliance with Israel was apparently meant to create a new formula of deterrence for Iran, should the United States return to the deal. A further factor is the declining importance of the Palestinian issue in the wake of the repercussions of the Arab Spring and the Covid-19 pandemic, which focused the attention of Arab states on domestic priorities. This declining importance led to the final factor: the relative indifference on the part of Arab and Muslim states to the UAE initiative to normalise relations with Israel, which in turn bolstered other rulers' confidence, triggering a domino effect.

Still, tensions in East Jerusalem (over evictions from Sheikh Jarrah and clashes during Ramadan on the Haram al-Sharif/Temple Mount), followed by the Israel–Hamas confrontation in May of this year – the bloodiest clash since the Gaza war of 2014 – had a clearly negative impact.

The establishment of diplomatic relations between Israel and the UAE, Bahrain, Sudan and Morocco are the product of long-term processes, coupled with the coincidence of mutual interests and an American president eager to leave his mark. These developments led to some significant results. First, Israel's position in the Middle East has been transformed; it currently maintains diplomatic or secret relations with at least thirteen Arab states, in addition to Turkey and several minorities. Second, many actors no longer fear the repercussions of exposing their relations with

> *Yet "peace for peace" is a misleading formula*

Israel, which is recognised as a useful partner against common enemies. Three, the recent agreements offer a new kind of relations: while the treaties with Egypt and Jordan produced a "cold peace" held between governmental agencies and based predominantly on mutual national security interests, the peace with the new Arab partners offers a warmer version, based on civilian, economic and cultural cooperation. Normalisation, which has a negative connotation in Arabic (*tatbi'*), has now gained a more positive flavour, which might affect other peace agreements in the long run.

Trump's moves to achieve Israeli–Arab deals were enthusiastically received by Netanyahu and the Israeli right, which attempted to market them under the slogan "peace for peace". This new "concept" was meant to convey to the Israeli public that the old formula of "land for peace" is no longer relevant or necessary. Though the idea of annexing territories in the West Bank has been dropped – at least for now – as a result of domestic Israeli politics and Emirati insistence, right-wing Israelis interpreted these four normalisation deals as a green light to continue the settlement project, thus establishing yet more facts on the ground and making a two-state solution increasingly untenable.

Yet "peace for peace" is a misleading formula. Israel has no borders with the UAE, Bahrain, Sudan or Morocco, and has never waged war against these states. As much as Israel desires peace with Arab countries on the periphery, many people in Egypt, Jordan and elsewhere in the Arab world still oppose normalisation before the resolution of the Palestinian issue. According to some Arab polls, Israel is considered the major enemy, above Iran. Some Arab states (Saudi Arabia, Oman, Qatar, Kuwait) and Muslim states (Pakistan, Indonesia) have expressed opposition to normal relations with Israel prior to a solution – or at least major progress – on the Palestinian front. The Arab states that forged relations with Israel now have leverage over it, as any unreasonable actions (annexation, for example) would probably be met by Arab retaliation, such as recalling ambassadors, severing relations and more.

Thus, although Israel has transformed its position in the Middle East, the Palestinian issue remains a vital component of the conflict and cannot simply be bypassed. For Israel, the strong imperative to make peace with the Palestinians remains, especially given the demographic forecast that Palestinians from the Jordan River to the Mediterranean, currently almost equal in number to the Jews, will soon outnumber them, threatening the very notion of a "Jewish democratic state".

To solve the Israeli–Palestinian conflict, the two sides need to want an agreement and be willing to work for it. This was the lesson from the peace deal between Israel and Egypt, which began with secret contacts in Morocco in 1977 and led to Sadat's visit to Jerusalem; from the deal between Israel and Jordan's King Hussein in 1994; and from the Oslo agreements with the PLO. On the other hand, no fewer than eight American peace plans have been presented and failed: the Reagan Plan (1982), the Shultz Initiative (1988), the Clinton Parameters (2000), the Bush Road Map (2003), the Kerry Parameters (2016), and the Trump Peace Plan (2020). When both sides of the conflict had legitimate leaders who expressed willingness to take risks, and a measure of trust existed between them – only then could a skilled and committed third-party mediator bring peace. Unfortunately, the political situation on both sides of the Israel–Palestine conflict at present does not augur well for its resolution.

Though Israel's place in the Middle East has dramatically improved since its establishment, the recent war in Gaza and the riots inside Israel confirmed that further progress is likely to be difficult and unsteady until the long-running Palestinian problem is finally addressed. ≡

## Simon of Trent: How a lie becomes a "fact"

# Magda Teter

In 1493, a renowned Nuremberg printer, Anton Koberger, published *Liber Chronicorum*, commonly known as the *Nuremberg Chronicle*. Written by Hartmann Schedel, a German physician and historian, the chronicle purported to present an account of history from "the beginning of the world to our own time". Nothing like it had ever been printed before. The biggest attraction was "its pictures of famous men and cities" in thousands of woodcut images. The reader would think they were "not reading a series of stories but looking at them with [their] own eyes".

One of the most elaborate stories in the chronicle appeared towards the end, under the year 1475. It told of the disappearance and death of Simon, a toddler, during the Easter week in 1475, leading to one of the most notorious anti-Jewish trials in European history. The story was accompanied by an intricate woodcut depicting the "Blessed Simon of Trent" – an unusually large image, more than half the height of the page. The woodcut features a gruesome scene in which nine menacing Jews are shown in the act of killing a boy, Simon, in Trent, a town in northern Italy at the foot of the Alps. Simon's body is stretched in a cruciform, his blood flowing into a basin. The Jews are all named: Moyses, Angelus, Vita, Seligman, Mayr, Samuel, Thobias, Israhel, and Gruneta (although this was a printer's error: the name should be

Brunetta). This woodcut is one of the earliest representations of Jews in printed books.

The trial of the Trent Jews resulted in executions and conversions and effectively wiped out the town's tiny Jewish community. It was not the first persecution of Jews accused of killing a Christian child, but it had the most lasting influence on Jewish and Catholic history, canon law and anti-Jewish iconography. Accounts of it continue to circulate today.

The tale of Jews killing Christian children emerged in the twelfth century, when an English monk, Thomas of Monmouth, blamed Jews for the death of a twelve-year-old boy, William, whose body was found in 1144 in a forest near Norwich. In Thomas's tale, composed decades after William's death, local Jews had killed him in a re-enactment of Jesus's Passion. Throughout the European continent in the thirteenth century, these tales transformed into a far more pernicious and tenaciously rooted accusation that Jews killed Christian children to obtain their blood – an accusation that came to be known as the blood libel. This was the charge levelled against the Jews of Trent.

When two-year-old Simon did not return home on the Thursday night before Easter, people suspected that he had drowned in one of Trent's many canals. Such accidents were common in premodern Europe, when children were often left alone to go about or play. But rumours quickly spread, pinning the blame on the local Jews. Their houses were inspected on the Saturday, but nothing suspicious was found. The next day, 26 March 1475 – Easter Sunday and the fourth day of Passover – Simon's body washed up in a canal flowing under the house of a prominent Jew named Samuel. He was arrested, along with other Jews.

The local prince-bishop, Johannes Hinderbach, who held both ecclesiastical and secular power, recognised that the town had an opportunity to benefit from Simon's death. The year 1475 was a jubilee year in the Catholic Church, and pilgrims were streaming towards Rome. If Simon was killed by Jews, then the boy was a holy martyr, his body a relic and an attraction for pilgrims who would stop in his town. So, even before the trial's interrogations began, the narrative of Simon's martyrdom was prepared. The boy's body was displayed as a holy relic in a church for visitors to see.

While previous anti-Jewish accusations had remained part of local lore, Bishop Hinderbach recognised that the recently invented printing press enabled such claims to be publicised far beyond his own town. An avid buyer and consumer of books, which he read and profusely annotated, Hinderbach deployed this new print technology to popularise Simon's cult, its validity hinging on affirming the Jews' culpability. He arranged for the printing of illustrated broadsides, popular and inexpensive publications printed on one side of large sheets of paper, as well as books and pamphlets, which were all disseminated far more widely than manuscript chronicles or hand-painted images ever could have been.

Hinderbach invested in publicising the story – in rhyme and prose, in visual art such as paintings and sculpture, and in printed text and image, which allowed for the distribution of a flood of publications that, for the first time, made the medieval tale of "Jewish murders of Christian children" imaginable through a powerful narrative coupled with visual representation. No fewer than thirty-three publications about Simon appeared in print between 1475 and 1500, not counting instances where the story was included in works of wider scope, such as Hartmann Schedel's 1493 *Nuremberg Chronicle*.

Hinderbach thus devised the first multimedia propaganda campaign aimed at reaching broad audiences across Europe. No other anti-Jewish libel, before or after, inspired such rich literary and artistic production. And no other had a comparable impact on European history.

Hinderbach's efforts did not go unchallenged. Pope Sixtus IV objected to the trial, following the example of his predecessors who had condemned blood accusations against Jews since 1247. The pope also feared that a new pilgrimage shrine could be idolatrous, if not properly vetted. He thus prohibited the veneration of Simon. Hinderbach and his supporters ignored the pope's objections and continued spending money to promote the story and the shrine, sponsoring devotional art and printed works.

Following Hinderbach's death in 1486, these efforts diminished. But by then, literature and art about Simon and the trial had already shaped the visual vocabulary of blood accusations against Jews, especially in northern Europe – where, as Schedel's chronicle shows, the literary and pictorial representations emphasised the cruelty of the Jews. In Italy, the taste for iconography was different, and tended to be more theological. Instead of depicting Jews in the act of murdering Simon, the dominant imagery emphasised Simon's "holy" status, with Jews almost entirely missing.

The broadsides and pamphlets depicting Jews murdering Simon made their way across the Alps, including to Nuremberg, where the magnificent chronicle was being prepared. One of these broadsides from 1475, now largely forgotten, inspired the intricate image of Simon in the *Nuremberg Chronicle*.

Simon's story and other similar tales entered other chronicles and cosmographies. Such repetition and inclusion in respectable publications turned a story grounded in a lie into an accepted historical "fact". The most virulent and ultimately deadly antisemitism in modern times would develop and take root in northern and eastern Europe – also the regions where anti-Jewish iconography emphasised Jewish cruelty.

Although the image from Schedel's 1493 chronicle became *the* iconic image of "blood libel" or "ritual murder" in modern times, there is no evidence that it had much cultural significance in the early modern period. In fact, between 1493 and the end of the eighteenth century, only one source among hundreds citing Simon's story referred to Schedel's work. The image from Schedel's chronicle had clearly been forgotten.

The now iconic woodcut reappeared at the beginning of the twentieth century in an obscure German publication, but then received a new lease on life under the Nazi regime, when a facsimile edition of the *Nuremberg Chronicle* was published in Leipzig in 1933. This spurred the widespread Nazi use of that image in their propaganda, beginning in 1934 in the antisemitic tabloid *Der Stürmer*. After that, it was republished in books and pamphlets in Germany, Italy and Poland to justify Nazi policies against Jews. And today, the image of Simon of Trent in the *Nuremberg Chronicle* continues to appear repeatedly in modern scholarly and antisemitic publications with little understanding of its forgotten history and context.

The transmission of Simon's story provides cautionary lessons about the power of images, the spread of fake tales and lies, and the importance of individuals and leadership in history. Without Bishop Hinderbach's investment of time, energy and money, Simon's story might have faded away like many other medieval tales. The bishop's determination and his deployment of a new mass media technology allowed this story to spread, influencing the way these anti-Jewish accusations were subsequently told, depicted and remembered, and rooting them deeply in the European Christian imagination.

In April 2019, a white supremacist shooter attacked a synagogue in California near San Diego, killing one and wounding many others. In his online "manifesto", he listed among his motivations to kill Jews "Simon of Trent, the horror that you and countless children have endured at the hands of the Jews". These stories, disseminated widely through early printed chronicles and appropriated and amplified in the twentieth century by the Nazis, have found fertile ground among contemporary antisemites. They show how difficult it is to uproot a lie when it has been carefully planted and artfully tended. ▤

## The Jews of Kaifeng

# Nancy Berliner

When I was a kid in the 1960s, my father – who would never pass up an opportunity to tell a good joke, or a bad one – had a string of stories that linked Jews and Chinese people, often preposterously. At that time, in our minds, China was as far away as one could go from anything Jewish, and he populated his stories with Chinese waiters speaking Yiddish at kosher delis, elderly Jewish men speaking Chinese on cruise ships, and everything in between.

I grew up to become a sinologist. And lived for years in Beijing.

One day, an Israeli friend – a specialist in Chinese literature who spoke Chinese fluently – came to Beijing for research. During a taxi ride, the driver swivelled around and, seeing his passenger was a foreigner, asked where he came from.

"Israel," my friend answered proudly.

"Aha!" the driver said. "Then you must be Jewish!"

My friend answered in the affirmative, to which the driver replied, "You know, there used to be many Jews in China."

My friend had heard the line too many times. "There are more people who have written about the Jews of China than there ever were Jews in China," he replied dryly.

"Well," the driver said, "I am Jewish." And he proceeded to tell the story of the Jews of Kaifeng.

My topic here is not just the story of the Jews of Kaifeng – as my friend rightly noted, they have been analysed from all angles. My topic is: why is this community so interesting? What draws us to their story? After all, there are Jews in the United States, in France, in Tunisia – why not China?

But first, I'll share a little background about this community.

*

Their story begins 2500 years ago, with the exile of Jews from Jerusalem to Babylon, today's Iraq. Many of these displaced people were traders. They travelled far and wide with their merchandise, following the demands of the market and settling in lands further east. They were drawn to the *suqs* of Persia, Afghanistan, Samarkand, India and, eventually, China.

Evidence of Jews in China dates back to at least the Tang dynasty (618–907). Scraps of paper with Hebrew prayers and letters in Judeo-Persian have been found at sites along the old trading routes in what is now north-western China. These snippets must have been dropped or lost by travelling merchants. But around the eleventh century, a substantial number of Judeo-Persian-speaking Jews settled in the then capital city, Bianliang, now called Kaifeng. They most likely came from India, selling cotton. The emperor welcomed them, allowing them to make their home in his cosmopolitan metropolis and offering them eight Chinese surnames.

By 1163, the community had grown large enough to construct a significant synagogue to conduct their rituals and house their Torahs. During the fifteenth, sixteenth and seventeenth centuries, the community erected monumental stone steles to record for future generations their practices, their beliefs and their history, as they understood it. The steles were, in effect, the start of the flood of writings about the Kaifeng Jews.

*

Europeans only became aware of, and began writing about, the Kaifeng community in the early seventeenth century. An educated Kaifeng Jew, Ai Tian, travelled to the Ming capital, Beijing, a journey of about 600 kilometres. Having heard a rumour that a foreigner was there, practising an unusual religion, Ai sought him out, thinking a co-religionist had landed in China. Alas, the foreigner was a Christian, the Jesuit priest Matteo Ricci. The Italian tried to explain to the puzzled Jew that the Messiah, Jesus, had arrived. Ai refused to accept Ricci's historiography, and returned to Kaifeng disappointed. Matteo Ricci meanwhile sent a communiqué back to Europe, sparking great curiosity. A hundred years later, another European Jesuit, Father Jean-Paul Gozani, made the arduous expedition to Kaifeng and wrote a full report, complete with sketches and descriptions of the synagogue and the worship practices within. His account set off a parade of investigations and writings about the Jews of Kaifeng, a rich and colourful procession – including a completely fictional novel, *Peony*, by Pearl Buck in 1948 – that continues today.

By the time Kaifeng had become more accessible to the inquisitive Europeans, religious activity and knowledge had begun to fade among the city's Jews. The last rabbi had passed away in the early nineteenth century, the economic situation had declined, and there were no funds to rebuild the deteriorating synagogue. Impoverished, they sold their Torahs and manuscripts to Europeans eager to find prophesies of Christ in what they thought were ancient, unabridged versions of the text. (To their dismay, the texts of Chinese Torahs were the same as those elsewhere.) The many manuscripts brought back to Europe – including Passover Haggadot and prayer books – all testify to the rich Jewish textual life maintained in Kaifeng for about 800 years. They also provide fodder for scholars to try to reconstruct the lifestyle of Jews who, for centuries, were isolated from other members of their faith.

For many years, the 625-page tome *Chinese Jews* by the bishop William Charles White, published in 1944, was considered the most comprehensive study. The Anglican bishop lived in Kaifeng as a missionary from 1910 to 1930. He became fascinated with the city's Jews and acquired an assemblage of objects from the local community, which he collected for the Royal Ontario Museum, where they are still housed and displayed.

An oft-reproduced photograph from White's book features two men facing a Torah scroll encased in a tall, cylindrical *tiq*, the container commonly used by Asian Jewish communities for storing Torahs. The *tiq* sits on a nineteenth-century Chinese chair. One man is of Asian appearance. He dons a round hat, a long white robe and cotton shoes. The other, with his back to us, wears a conical hat, a turban and a white robe under a darker *magua*, a type of short, loose Chinese jacket. The implication is that here are two Jewish Chinese men reading the sacred text. Yet Sara Irwin, former director of collections at the Royal Ontario Museum, who has written thorough studies of the Judaica objects White collected, recently shared a little-known secret about this photograph: one of the men is the bishop himself, the other his assistant. While the bishop researched and presented – and partially concocted – a narrative of the Jews of Kaifeng, Irwin adds, his texts reveal that his ultimate agenda, like many others writing on the subject, was to convert these Jews to Christianity.

European Christians were not the only ones to write about the Jews of Kaifeng. As early as 1910, the Chinese scholar Zhang Xiangwen researched and published the texts engraved on the stone steles. Chinese historians have continued to delve into these texts. And many Jewish sinologists, including the eminent Berthold Laufer, curator of Asian ethnology at the Chicago Field Museum, and Benjamin Schwartz, my own first professor of Chinese intellectual history at Harvard, could not resist the temptation to dive into the subject. In 1999, China scholar Professor Donald Leslie, who died last year at the age of ninety-eight, published a 291-page bibliography on the Jews of China.

Four years ago, I met David Stern and Kathryn Hellerstein, a powerhouse academic couple in the world of Jewish studies. Hellerstein is the director of the Jewish Studies program at University of Pennsylvania, and a professor of Germanic languages, specialising in Yiddish; Stern is a professor of classical and modern Jewish and Hebrew literature at Harvard. Though not obvious from their titles, both are deeply involved in the realms of Jewish China. On a snowy evening, my partner and I dined with the pair in an elegant restaurant in Cambridge. Hellerstein explained that she was organising, with Chinese colleagues Xu Xin and Song Lihong of the Glazer Institute for Jewish and Israel Studies at Nanjing University, an academic conference in Nanjing, with a focus on Ashkenazi Jews in China. Among the participants were a Chinese Talmudic scholar, a Chinese translator of Isaac Bashevis Singer's novels, and the director of the Shanghai Jewish Refugees Museum. She invited me to deliver a paper.

During our meal, Stern showed me a photocopy of a page of Hebrew and Chinese text from a seventeenth-century document. I was beyond delighted to see, for the first time, tangible evidence of these two ancient cultures intersecting so naturally on one sheet of paper. Having spent a large chunk of my life immersed in China, I saw my two identities – as a Jew and a China scholar – merging. The page was from a booklet listing Kaifeng synagogue congregants, men and women, their names written in Chinese and Hebrew. I excitedly pointed out where, under the Hebrew for *Moshe*, the scribe had noted *jinshi* in neat, brushed Chinese characters, indicating that the Jewish-Chinese gentleman had passed the highest level of civil examinations in Beijing. The 76-page booklet is now in the library of the Hebrew Union College in Cincinnati. Laufer, the esteemed sinologist, first saw the booklet in 1927, and later wrote of his own emotional response: "The mere fact that it was the only Chinese-Hebrew manuscript I had ever laid my hands on, and presumably the only one in existence, proved a magnetic attraction in itself."

Stern's photocopy reminded me of the day I was in a dusty, state-owned used bookshop in Beijing, when my eyes randomly fell on a peculiarly sized, well-thumbed string-bound paperback. It was, the store's manager explained, an Esperanto–Chinese dictionary, published in 1924. "I'll take it," I said without hesitation. The memory of my visit to the Polish town of Białystok flashed into my mind, the guide pointing out the "home" of Dr L.L. Zamenhof, the Jewish ophthalmologist who invented Esperanto in the late nineteenth century. (In fact, the house is no longer there.) What inspired me to flip through the pages to the word for Palestine? *Palastin-o* was defined there in Chinese as the "old Jewish country, now a possessed territory" – possessed by the British, presumably, given the date of publication. Those few Chinese characters recognising the existence of Jews warmed me. The book had multiple intersections of China and Jews, all of which made China less foreign for me – just a place down the road from Israel, across Asia, where so many of my forebears had travelled before me.

Recently I stumbled across a 170-year-old Hebrew letter on the internet – our only means of travel during these Covid days. Sold at a Sotheby's "Important Judaica" sale in 2010, the letter was penned to the Jews of Kaifeng on the twenty-fifth day of the month of Heshvan, in the year 5611 (1850), by Isaac Faraj ben Reuben ben Jacob, a Baghdadi Jew who had settled in Shanghai four years earlier. Like the Kaifeng Jews, this Isaac was probably a descendant of the Jews exiled to Babylon, and like them had arrived in China as a merchant. He asks his long-lost relatives if they have a Torah or other Jewish texts, and whether the Shanghai Jewish community could send them anything. Whether the Kaifeng Jews received or understood the letter is not known. Nineteenth-century Christian visitors to Kaifeng noted that Jews there claimed they could no longer read Hebrew. Nevertheless, in time, at the invitation of the Baghdadi Jews in Shanghai, several Kaifeng Jews went to Shanghai to learn Hebrew and Jewish rituals.

*

Here we are in 5781, or 2021, learning to be more sensitive to the diversity of our communities. The Kaifeng Jews remind us that not all Jews go back to the shtetls of Eastern Europe. Isaac Faraj ben Reuben ben Jacob knew that, and probably never considered those distant shtetls. My boyfriend, who is of Baghdadi-Jewish descent, knows that as well (and groans when people assume he understands Yiddish).

In Kaifeng, Jews worshipped in buildings with upturned eaves and lotus-decorated bowls. Will future Jews be charmed that American Jews pray in our mid-century modern shuls, (or, shall

we say, *qingzhensi*, "temples of purity and truth", as the Kaifeng
Jews called their places of worship, using the same term local
Muslims employed for their places of worship)? My father would
have smiled. ▤

---

## Too much past

**Deborah Levy**

**In Memory of Memory**
*Maria Stepanova*
*Fitzcarraldo Editions, 2020*

When the pandemic roared into the end of the second decade of our twenty-first century, the past become livelier in my mind. With the present and the future both in flux, it was as if I had nowhere else to go. During the long days and nights of various lockdowns, I wondered if the past was rudely visiting me, ghostly, uninvited, or if I was walking backwards, uninvited, to haunt it.

The main soundtrack in my life at this time was the wailing sirens of ambulances taking Covid-19 patients to hospital. Maybe because death was in the air, I found myself revisiting Chekhov's great play *Three Sisters*, first performed in 1901 at the Moscow Art Theatre. When I was a theatre student, age nineteen, a famous female director came to our college to create a production of this play, and I was cast as melancholy, rebellious Masha. I suspect the director thought my high cheekbones suited the role, but alas, I had little acting talent. With hindsight (not my favourite sort of sight), maybe the director did not have much directing talent either.

These spirited sisters, Olga, Masha and Irina, all of them in their twenties, live on the edge of a small provincial Russian town.

After the death of their parents, the sisters' most fierce desire is to go back to cosmopolitan, cultured Moscow, where they were born. They love the past more than they love the present, and wish to return to it.

On the night of the first performance, I sat on the stage chaise longue in full costume, staring blankly into space, while Olga, my stage sister, spoke the first line: "It's exactly a year ago today that Father died, the fifth of May." That this play begins on the anniversary of Masha, Olga and Irina's father's death did not mean very much to me at the age of nineteen. In fact, it seems to me now, age sixty, that all of us young actors were trying to create an emotional mood we did not yet understand.

Why, I asked myself, as another ambulance rattled down the road, did the director not say to that cast of young people: "May I ask if any of you have experienced the death of a parent?" And if just one of us had replied, "Yes, my mother died when I was twelve," the director would have been wise to ask if that student might share some of the thoughts and feelings that come out to play on the anniversary of a parent's death. That way, I would not have been staring blankly into space on the night of the first performance.

And something else. Masha quotes from Pushkin at the start of the play: "A green oak by the curving shore, and on that oak a chain of gold." I sort of understood those lines, age nineteen, but I did not feel them. Later, maybe thirty years later, when my marriage was on the rocks (as was Masha's in *Three Sisters*), I read Sylvia Plath's poem "The Couriers": "A ring of gold with the sun in it? Lies. Lies and a grief." Oh, I thought, so *that's* what Masha was trying to convey.

As the Danish philosopher Søren Kierkegaard told us, "Life can only be understood backwards; but it must be lived forwards."

That ring of gold came back again, in a different form, when I joined a queue one day outside a London grocery store, all of us wearing surgical masks – as if they were the most normal accessory in the world. Someone in the queue asked me if I "had the time". It's a perfectly reasonable question, but the pandemic had somehow managed to congeal time, and anyway, these days everyone has the time on their phones. I found myself looking at my wrist, as if I had a watch strapped to it, which I did not. This gesture, glancing at a watch that was not there, brought back to me the memory of the little gold watch my paternal grandmother, who was born in Krekenava, Lithuania, bequeathed to me. I was seven when she died, and it fitted my wrist perfectly.

Her name was Miriam Leah. When she arrived in Cape Town, age twelve, in 1908, it was changed to Mary. Her future husband's name was Abraham Moses and he changed it to Mark. Mary and Mark. I still think of my grandmother as Miriam Leah, though I understand that Mary was her avatar to survive antisemitism. She was Mary like Mary Poppins, except she spoke English with a Yiddish accent. I'm not sure what happened to that watch. I must have lost it.

That afternoon, queueing to buy apricots, I realised that what I had inherited was not a "grown-up" watch, as I had thought at seven, but a child's watch. It would not have fitted even the dainty wrists of Mary/Miriam when she was an adult woman.

Did Miriam Leah travel with that watch on the long journey from Lithuania to Cape Town? Why did I never ask her about that journey? Or, to put it another way, why was I not pointed by my family to ask her about the epic journey she made with Rosa, her older sister? The train, the ship, the suitcases carried in a cart pulled by horses. Their mother had died of cancer and so the two sisters were obliged to join their estranged father in South Africa.

I would guess that Rosa and Miriam felt a bit tender on the anniversary of their mother's death. They would know how to speak the line, "It's exactly a year ago today that Mother died." What happened to Miriam/Mary's relatives and the family friends who remained in Lithuania? Apparently my grandmother told my father stories about the pogroms she had witnessed in her village, yet as an adult, he says, she never spoke of the Holocaust. That silence was transmitted to me, too. I know nothing about my extended family in Lithuania. It is a silence I explore in my novel *Swimming Home:* "If cities map the past with statues made from bronze forever frozen in one dignified position, as much as I try to make the past keep still and mind its manners, it moves and murmurs with me through every day."

All the same, why is that gold watch important to me? What do I really want to know about it and what is it there to do?

This is one of the many questions that Maria Stepanova, Russian poet and writer of exquisite long-form prose, asks herself in her book *In Memory of Memory*, a 500-page deep dive into historical, cultural and personal memory. In a sense, she answers it in one punchy line: "There comes a day when the scattered pieces of knowledge need to be fixed in a transmission line."

Stepanova begins this discursive, epic meditation, beautifully translated by Sasha Dugdale, on and around the ways in which her "ordinary" Jewish family managed to survive the persecutions of the twentieth century, with the death of her father's estranged sister. The narrator finds herself in Aunt Galya's apartment, sorting through postcards, ivory brooches, photographs, letters, diaries, souvenirs. She realises that this hoard is a valuable archive of the twentieth century. "Objects from the long distant past," Stepanova writes, "look as if they have been caught in the headlights, they're awkward, embarrassingly naked. It's as if they have nothing left to do."

Stepanova is at her most searing when she writes about the "nonhuman face" of objects. Her description of missing parts of crockery as "orphaned", or faded photographs as "foundlings", opens the mind and lets in our own personal and historical associations. She is particularly astute on family photographs, noting there is always one that features "a middle-aged, stylish woman, suffering from chronic, mild depression".

Many writers are called upon to accompany Stepanova on what is as much a thought experiment "on the way memory works, and what memory wants from me" as an attempt to piece together shattered fragments of family history. These writers include Sebald, Proust, Barthes, Nabokov, Sontag and, perhaps most piercingly, Osip Mandelstam, under the heading "The Jewboy hides from view".

A few visual artists are enlisted too, but less successfully. Stepanova includes a short, rather basic treatise on the extraordinary photography of Francesca Woodman, who experimented with ways of making herself blur and disappear in her self-portraits. Woodman suicided in 1981, age twenty-two. She is twinned with the vibrant, turbulent, ironic paintings of Charlotte Salomon, who was murdered age twenty-six in Auschwitz. Stepanova writes in a chapter entitled "Selfies and their consequences", "All that disappears is what made you yourself." Is that true?

It is certainly true for the narrator in W.G. Sebald's 2001 novel, *Austerlitz*. He gradually discovers the fate of his mother, who was deported to the death camps. There is a great deal at stake for Jacques Austerlitz. This is because he carries within himself knowledge that is too painful to access. His assignment with the past is to recover this knowledge.

Stepanova's narrator speaks and thinks in a detached, elegant, serene tone. Perhaps there is no other tone that can better handle the panorama of ideas she puts to work in this philosophical investigation into remembering and forgetting. If I am not sure what is at stake, or what her narrator wants to know, or even what it is she wishes to unknow, perhaps that's her point. "There is too much past, and everyone knows it," she tells us. As her title suggests, memory itself is an artefact. Stepanova is astute on the spectres that haunt Europe, too.

In contemporary Europe, with its barely healed wounds, black holes, and traces of displacement, a well-preserved family archive is a rarity. A set of furniture and china that has come together over decades, inherited from aunts and grandmothers and once thought of as an ancient burden, now deserves its own special memorial. Those who were forced to flee (it hardly matters from whom they fled) burnt documents, shredded photographs, cut off everything below the chin – officer epaulettes, army greatcoats, civil service uniforms – and left their papers with other people. By the end of the journey very little is left for the memory to cling to, and to set sail on.

It is sometimes a relief in this dense, intense, meandering stretch of writing to come across an anchoring line, such as "My grandfather was from the southern port city of Odessa." And a pleasure to learn that the cab drivers in Odessa "sang opera arias as if they were gondoliers". At the same time, the narrator tells us, "News of pogroms spread like wildfire around Southern Ukraine. It travelled on trains with the railwaymen, down the Dniepr with the ferrymen, jostled at hiring fairs, and served as a model for new outbursts of pointless cruelty: 'Let's do it the Kievan way!'"

Towards the end of the massive achievement that is *In Memory of Memory*, Stepanova writes, "Sometimes it seems like it is only possible to love the past if you know it is definitely never going to return." I know what she means. Chekhov understood this too. The three sisters do not return to Moscow. Miriam Leah did not return to Lithuania. Yet, as Freud told us, the past does return, and though we might wish to see it off, the repressed will jump into the queue at the grocery store and present itself in the form of a child's gold watch. Memory was Freud's major subject, of course, a life's work. His archaeological metaphor suggests that to recover the past, with all its shards and fragments, we have to dig down and bring to the surface those memories that have been pushed out of consciousness. And so, for this reader anyway, the unconscious of *In Memory of Memory* is the way it obsessively digs up the perilous twentieth century and searches among its tram routes, crockery and stockings for the trauma wound.

The past is not exactly a stranger at our table, but it is uncanny all the same. Neither dead nor alive, it does not return my stares or smiles or tears, but in my own mind it does listen to my thoughts. Somehow, I believe we are both of us the present and the past, slightly altered from this exchange of knowledge and feeling. ▤

# The collectors

## Anne Sebba

**House of Fragile Things: A History of Jewish
Art Collectors in France, 1870–1945**
*James McAuley*
*Yale University Press, 2021*

**Letters to Camondo**
*Edmund de Waal*
*Chatto & Windus, 2021*

There is a story of Cardinal Mazarin, the seventeenth-century French diplomat who, from 1642 until his death in 1661, served two kings of France, Louis XIII and Louis XIV. Walking among his possessions shortly before he died, he muttered unhappily: "All this must be left behind." The prospect of relinquishing a painstakingly acquired collection taunts many collectors.

Why did so many immensely wealthy French Jews lovingly amass vast collections of treasures at the end of the nineteenth and early twentieth centuries, if only to give them away? What did they hope to achieve and why, in the end, did they fail? These are just some of the questions James McAuley, former Paris correspondent for the *Washington Post*, probes in *The House of Fragile Things*. It is a riveting and devastating account of a battle between the cultured and sophisticated *fin de siècle* Parisian art world – mostly but not exclusively Jewish – and the brutal greed of the Nazis, aided by the long-standing antisemitism of their French collaborators. McAuley recognises that, on one level, the collections (and now the museums) this Jewish elite left behind were attempts to create something beautiful in the increasingly hostile environment of the country they loved. But it is much more complicated than that.

From 1806 onwards, as post-revolution France became the first country in Western Europe to emancipate the Jews, Jewish people from less enlightened countries flocked there in pursuit of its democratic ideals. Mostly they flourished, but they also encountered the antisemitism that burst into the international consciousness with the Dreyfus affair, "when the very notion of Frenchness was more fiercely contested than ever before as France had repeatedly swung between revolution and reaction, republic and restoration". It was at this moment in history that "the fight for the objects from a nation's storied past became a battle for the soul of a nation – who it belonged to but also who belonged to it".

In his rigorously researched book, McAuley skilfully traces the effect of this multi-layered migration into a country where, alongside the Enlightenment, there also existed a robust tradition of antisemitism. He evokes the "vanished and rarefied world" of French Jews in the upper echelons of society as an entire universe, at the centre of which was the Camondo family – now obliterated, even if their collections and mansion survive. The Camondos lived close to, married into, and had lives interwoven with those of the Reinach, Rothschild, Ephrussi and Cahen d'Anvers families. In their enemies' eyes, they were not only cousins, but emblematic of Jews (or, in the parlance of the time, *Israélites*) intruding where they did not belong. More and more, they all had to face down critics such as the Goncourt brothers – after whom the prestigious French literary prize is named – who denounced their collecting activities as *bricabracomania*. The virulently antisemitic journalist Édouard Drumont went further, claiming that collecting was a criminal act of Jewish violence, and hunting was such an ancient right that if Jews took part it would constitute trespassing. It was only in the private spaces these families created that "they had total control and absolute authority, a security they never enjoyed in the outside world".

The Camondos were a fabulously wealthy banking family from Constantinople. As religiously observant oriental Jews who had arrived in Paris in 1869, they did not enjoy the same status in Franco-Jewish society as the predominantly Ashkenazi elite. In 1891, 31-year-old Moïse de Camondo married nineteen-year-old Irène Cahen d'Anvers, who was Paris-born, both consolidating two important banking families and guaranteeing the social elevation of the Camondos in Parisian society. But by 1903, the couple were divorced, a public scandal and private humiliation for Moïse, as Irène abandoned her husband for the family's Italian Catholic stable master, Count Carlo Sampieri. From then on, Moïse used his house as a place of retreat where he brought up his son, Nissim, and daughter, Béatrice.

From the moment he inherited 63 Rue de Monceau from his father, Moïse removed all traces of the exotic Levantine culture to which his parents had cleaved. He sought instead to create a quintessentially French house, modelled specifically after Versailles' Petit Trianon and decorated exclusively in the late-eighteenth-century style he considered to be "one of the glories of France". His ambition was to purchase a certain image of Frenchness, which he hoped would soften the foreignness of the family name and thereby help to combat antisemitism.

To the point of obsession, provenance played a major role in what Moïse de Camondo chose to collect: he sought objects imbued with national significance. When dealers wrote to him offering pieces, however exquisite, from a period in which he was not interested, he would write back, politely rejecting them. He only bought Louis XVI furniture, believing that objects from this period were part of France's endangered national heritage and must be preserved. An item's possible association with the French royal family increased its value immeasurably, while an object that had some direct contact with Queen Marie Antoinette was a particularly sought-after prize.

After the humiliation of his divorce, Moïse suffered a far more terrible blow. In September 1917, his beloved son, a fighter in the French air force to whom he had intended to leave the house, went missing in action. In the days before Nissim's fate was known, Marcel Proust, who lived nearby, wrote a commiserating letter to Moïse. Once Nissim's death was confirmed, Moïse was grimly determined to reclaim his son's body and bring it back to France, despite the raging war and closed borders. According to McAuley, this is further proof that "he was a consummate collector, as he pursued his son's remains with more vigour than any other object he ever sought".

After Nissim's death, Moïse took his meals alone in the narrow "porcelain room", with only his Sèvres dinner service, *les services aux oiseaux Buffon*, displayed in glass-fronted cabinets, for company. Six years later, in 1923, following the departure of his daughter, Béatrice, and her husband, Léon Reinach, to a home of their own, he began to contemplate turning the house into a museum. Until that point, his primary purpose in collecting had been intensely personal and private.

Although McAuley focuses on the Camondos, he also discusses Léon's father, the formidable intellect, archaeologist and collector Théodore Reinach, who bequeathed his magnificent Greek-style Villa Kerylos in the French Riviera town of Beaulieu-sur-Mer to the Institut de France upon his death in 1928. Both men were using their magnificent homes to challenge the strain of French antisemitism that insisted Jews could never know true beauty or achieve aesthetic authenticity. One of the most interesting aspects of McAuley's book is his understanding that collecting in this way was almost exclusively a male activity. Many of the women in this opulent milieu felt doubly excluded – from collecting and from Judaism. In Judaism these women saw both the source and essence of the gendered power structures that governed every aspect of their lives, one factor in their subsequent conversion to Christianity.

Edmund de Waal, in his richly inventive book *Letters to Camondo*, is also drawn to the image of Moïse eating alone at a small table in the porcelain room. In de Waal's dreamlike volume of imagined letters, Moïse sits there, looking out the window at the gently swaying trees in his garden, and beyond into the Parc Monceau. "They are ash trees," de Waal writes to his "dear friend" – for, as he says, he is not entirely sure how to address Monsieur le Comte – "and were planted when your father and uncle moved here in 1870." De Waal is deeply familiar with the area through researching his Ephrussi ancestors, whom he wrote about so lovingly in *The Hare with Amber Eyes*. They arrived in Paris from Odessa, also in 1869, and lived at number 8, ten houses up from the Hôtel Camondo. Now he turns his gaze on the Camondo family, since "everyone here … seems to be a cousin", wandering from room to room, idea to idea, and, like McAuley, spending hours in the meticulously preserved fifth-floor archives, from which he learns some telling details. Once Moïse decided that the house was to become a museum, he left detailed instructions as to how it was to be maintained, including a complete vacuum cleaning system "which works cheaply and marvellously well … but is too powerful for antique carpets, tapestries and silks". There are also directives for what must never be moved: he wanted "the photographs of my son which you find in diverse places in the house to stay always in those actual places".

De Waal discovers that, in 1933, Moïse donated to the Musée des Arts Decoratifs an entire collection of fifty-five tie pins given to his father, also named Nissim, by his American-born lover, the former Julia Tahl of Baltimore, who became the Comtesse de Lancey. Three years later, on 21 December 1936, there was a ceremony to hand over the entire house and collection to the same museum, part of the Louvre.

Yet for all that the archives reveal about objects and prices paid, they contain little that is personal. The story of the family's tragic destruction following the Nazi occupation in 1940 must be told by both authors mostly by way of bureaucratic documents and the occasional letter. Béatrice writes to a friend insisting that she is "miraculously protected" by God and the Virgin Mary. Nonetheless, in 1944, by then divorced and converted to Catholicism, she was deported – first to Drancy, then to Auschwitz. She died there in January 1945, two weeks before the camp was liberated. Her still-Jewish ex-husband, Léon Reinach, and their two children, Fanny and Bertrand, had been murdered at Auschwitz in 1943.

Inevitably, there are gaps in the story, specifically personal details about Béatrice and why her marriage to Léon ended in divorce in 1942, as well what she did or did not know about the Nazis looting the family home. McAuley suspects that Léon, whose entire family had devoted their lives to removing barriers between being a loyal French patriot and an *Israélite*, could not stomach his wife's conversion to Catholicism, sincere or not. Yet, McAuley concludes, what remains unknown to us is Béatrice's secret, "the only property she still controls". Preserving at least something of the people and their world as they were "in the end … is all that matters". It is a haunting and tantalising conclusion, and McAuley is to be congratulated for giving readers and putative visitors to 63 Rue de Monceau a vivid sense of the people who created it. Ensuring that they will never be forgotten is a step in the continual attempt to make sense of things of which no sense can ever be made. But, much as I loved the passion of both these books, much as I too fell in love with the Camondo house on the first day I saw it some twenty years ago, I wonder – is it quite *all* that matters, or simply the best memorial we can offer them?

De Waal closes his book with a chapter about *La Petite Irène*, Renoir's 1880 portrait of a beautiful, blue-eyed, red-haired child that came to symbolise so much that was lost. Irène's mother, Louise Cahen d'Anvers, gave the portrait to her granddaughter Béatrice, and it hung in the Reinach apartment in Neuilly until Léon sent it for safekeeping to the Château de Chambord in 1939. It was confiscated by the Nazis, sent to Göring's country residence, then recovered after the war and shipped back to Paris, where it was displayed in 1946 as part of an exhibition of looted French masterpieces found in Germany. Irène Sampieri, the painting's subject, subsequently reclaimed it on behalf of her murdered daughter's estate, then sold it to Emil Bührle, a Swiss, whose armaments company supplied the Nazis. Today it hangs in the *Foundation E.G. Bührle* in Zurich.

De Waal quotes Walter Benjamin, the German-Jewish philosopher who died in 1940, describing the happiness of the collector as the "happiness of the solitary: tête-a-tête with things. Is not this the felicity that suffuses our memories – that in them we are alone with particular things … The collector 'stills' his fate. And that means he disappears in the worlds of memory." The Camondo and Reinach families have all but disappeared, but those "worlds of memory" continue to draw us in, and we are lucky to have these wonderful, thought-provoking books to help us make sense of them. ▤

# Correspondence

*"White insurrections: Antisemitism in America"*
*by Deborah E. Lipstadt*

## Joshua Shanes

Deborah Lipstadt has written a cogent analysis of the role of antisemitism in American white nationalism, arguing that not only are the two "inextricably linked", but in fact antisemitism constitutes the very "foundation stone" of white nationalism in America, lending it "pseudo-intellectual heft" and "logic". To this end, she cites the work of Eric Ward (as well as her own book) and gives a variety of examples of nineteenth- and twentieth-century European antisemitism, and then of white nationalism in America from the 1990s, culminating in Charlottesville and the January 6th insurrection. (I would have added Pittsburgh, where the murderer was motivated by white nationalist fears of Latino invasion orchestrated by Jews.)

While the role of antisemitism in contemporary white nationalism is indisputable, I would like to push back on the argument that it has always played this foundational role in American racism. America was founded upon white supremacy – it was literally and metaphorically built by African slaves on land taken from Native Americans whom settlers murdered en masse. Our legal system and social hierarchy are saturated with racism, including but hardly limited to the institution of slavery. After the Civil War, the basis of reconstruction was the reassertion of white supremacy and disregard for the intent of the constitutional amendments that extended civil and legal protections to former slaves. We have seen a similar backlash in our lifetimes to the accomplishments of the civil rights era.

Antisemitism played little to no role in any of this. As Eric Kaufmann has demonstrated, American nationalism has always been not civic but ethnic, based on a notion of whiteness that slowly grew to incorporate more people over time: first Germans, eventually Irish, and even Jews, although not without significant resistance against the latter two. This matters. While ignoring the role of antisemitism in white nationalism today undermines our ability to address it, particularly because we need to build alliances between minority groups facing this threat, it equally does not help to foreground Jews in a country that has historically not done so. Despite the presence of antisemitism in particular times and places in American history, Jews have largely benefited from the racial hierarchy here, and this too must be acknowledged in order to build those alliances and tackle white nationalism. The essay, unfortunately, does not acknowledge that most Jews have benefited from whiteness in ways that African Americans and others have not – individually, and especially structurally.

Finally, while Lipstadt nods to the mantra of "both sides" – although without citing any American examples of the alleged problem of left-wing antisemitism – she avoids the elephant in the room, namely Israel. Perhaps this is because most charges of antisemitism against the "left" ultimately land on anti-Zionism? Lipstadt has elsewhere been careful to allow "legitimate criticism" of Israel, but in practice this distinction so often disappears in response to Palestinian activism. This essay, however, has the necessary means to escape this problem and to identify instances of antisemitic anti-Zionism. Her discussion of Richard Spencer, for example, should note that he is an open Zionist, as are antisemites like John Hagee and Robert Jeffress. This can give us a window to complicate the relationship between Zionism, anti-Zionism and antisemitism, and her conclusion brings this home. Her penultimate paragraph summarising the tropes of antisemitism is spot on. When these tropes are applied to Israel in place of Rothschild, Soros or "the Jews" – or when Palestinian activists attack Jews or synagogues as a substitute for Israel, as happened in May of this year – we have crossed over to antisemitism.

Lipstadt's essay thereby lays the foundation for addressing both antisemitism and white nationalism – namely, the urgent need to build alliances with other minorities that focus on strengthening democracy and notions of American identity grounded in civic nationalism and equality. Disagreements about Israel in that coalition will have to be tolerated.

*Joshua Shanes is Associate Professor of Jewish Studies, and Director of the Arnold Center for Israel Studies, at the College of Charleston.*

# Jeffrey Herf

Deborah Lipstadt's "White insurrections" draws attention to the central role that antisemitism plays in contemporary right-wing extremism, and its bizarre but important connection to white racism. In Charlottesville in August 2017, the American press was perplexed that demonstrators opposed to dismantling monuments to Confederate leaders chanted "Jews will not replace us" and used torches reminiscent of Nazi parades as they marched past a synagogue. Lipstadt's important essay explores the connection between these two hatreds and presents the thesis that "antisemitism is the ideological foundation stone of the far right's racism". To those who maintain the commonly held view that Jews who raise the issue of antisemitism do so as an expression of their "white privilege" and as a Zionist tactic to deflect criticism of Israel, Lipstadt's thesis is absurd. It is not. Yet, to more firmly establish her theory, additional historical perspective is required.

For most of their histories, antisemitism and white supremacy constituted distinct and causally unrelated cultural traditions. Beyond the obvious fact that hatred of "others" reinforces xenophobia and prejudice, neither formed an ideological foundation for the other. Racism towards peoples of colour, and the belief in a connection between skin colour and intellectual inferiority – whether in the United States or in Britain and the European colonial powers – had multiple causes unrelated to the traditions of antisemitism. Likewise, the radical antisemitism of the Holocaust did not have origins in racism towards peoples of colour. Rather, before and during the Holocaust, antisemitism was part of a Western – first religious, then secular – tradition that was distinct from racism based on skin colour. If Lipstadt is correct that antisemitism now, for the first time, offers an ideological foundation for white racism, we need to ask why.

"White insurrections" stimulates the following hypothesis: The distinguishing feature of radical antisemitism before, during and since the Holocaust is a paranoid conspiracy theory that depicts first the Jews, and then the state of Israel, as powerful and evil, and engaged in efforts to dominate world politics in order to bring harm to millions of non-Jews. Those who apply this paranoid scheme to American history begin with the fact that American Jews and Jewish organisations and leaders, far more than their other white counterparts, supported African-American efforts to overcome the legacy of white racism. Jews are the only ethnic group among white Americans who have, by a vast majority, voted for the Democratic Party, especially as the Republican Party adopted the "Southern strategy" and increasingly became a party of white grievance.

White racists link black skin to intellectual and moral inferiority. They refuse to attribute the advance of African Americans into the professional middle classes, and then the election of Barack Obama as president, to the merits and qualifications of the individuals concerned. The political rise of Donald Trump, fuelled by lies about Obama's birth certificate, illustrated the depths of that racist conviction. The broad Jewish support for Obama lent support to the antisemitic argument that Jews were operating behind the scenes and were responsible for an otherwise inexplicable and threatening black advance. This intersectional, causal link fuses the antisemitic arguments about powerful and evil Jews with racist conviction of black inferiority. The antisemitic interpretation of black advance bonds the presumed unity of Jewish power and evil with the bundle of ideas that justified slavery and segregation. Trying to explain why the Allies were at war with Nazi Germany, Nazi propaganda minister Joseph Goebbels screamed that "the Jews are guilty". For the Nazis, antisemitism explained the inexplicable alliance of the Britain and the United States with the Soviet Union. Lipstadt's right-wing ideologues find that "the Jews are guilty" of something else altogether – the fact that African Americans have made significant social, economic and political advances in the last seventy years, and that the United States has become an increasingly multi-ethnic and multi-racial democracy, though efforts at voter suppression to undermine hard-won gains in voting rights persist.

The antisemitism of the extremist right solves the riddle of African American advance. It is the Jews who are "guilty" yet again, and who "betray" whites by seeking to "replace" white men especially, from their accustomed positions of power or privilege. The political implication of this paranoid fantasy is that violent attacks on Jews and Jewish institutions are necessary because, without the Jews, black Americans would be restored to the inferior and unequal status of second-class citizenship that the racist believes is the natural order of things.

The Lipstadt thesis is a starting point for further examination of these sensitive and crucial issues. There is more work to be done on the connections between antisemitism and white racism since the highpoint of the Civil Rights Movement in the 1960s. Importantly, Lipstadt has drawn attention to what seems at first a paradox. The clear implication of "White insurrections" is that in order to fight against white racism, we need also to fight against one of its ideological foundations, antisemitism.

*Jeffrey Herf, at the Department of History, University of Maryland, has published, among other works,* The Jewish Enemy: Nazi Propaganda During World War II and the Holocaust.

## Deborah Lipstadt responds

I appreciate Joshua Shanes' and Jeffrey Herf's observations on the historical nuances of the connection between American racism and antisemitism.

Shanes correctly contends that what we are seeing today is, at least to a certain extent, a relatively new phenomenon in American life. Racism in America, particularly in the post–Civil War period, was generally, though not always, separated from antisemitism. (Leo Frank would not have agreed.)

In a bitterly ironic fashion, however, they were linked. The presence of racism made Jews' lives "better". Jews often faced less antisemitism when they lived in places where there was another group that was more "other" – more different from whites – than they. Such was the case in the South, as well as in northern California, where Chinese people were the objects of opprobrium and disdain. It did not necessarily mean Jews were accepted; in the South they lived on tenterhooks, often waiting for the disaster that might well be lurking around the corner. (The same might be said of the apartheid-era South African Jewish community.) However, he is correct to note that what we are seeing today – this symbiotic relationship between antisemitism and racism – is a new development.

He also correctly notes that I should have added Pittsburgh to my litany of examples of the confluence of white nationalism and antisemitism. One could also add the attack on the synagogue in Poway in San Diego County (2019) and the synagogue in Halle, Germany (2019). One could go even further than that: Dylan Roof, who brutally murdered attendees at a Bible study session at Charleston's Emanuel African Methodist Episcopal Church, known among its parishioners as Mother Emanuel (2015), and Patrick Crusius, the murderer at the Walmart in El Paso (2019) intent on killing Latinos, were both motivated by the same sense of white nationalism that is inexorably linked to antisemitism. Tragically, this list only grows longer.

Herf correctly elaborates on the rationalisation, ludicrous as it might be, that Jews are the puppeteers using Black people to further their own goals. This notion has its roots in William Pierce's *The Turner Diaries*. Pierce hated Blacks and Jews. Incensed by the advances Blacks were making – at least from a legislative perspective – in voting rights, school access and housing opportunities, he looked for the culprits and found them among the Jews.

In the bitterest of ironies, and regarding a subject that was beyond my remit in the article, Herf notes how, in recent years, the argument posed by the far right – that Jews and Blacks are linked in a giant conspiracy aimed at destroying "white Christian" hegemony – has been joined by an equally absurd contention. This contention, emanating from the radical left, is that Jews are the cause of much of Black suffering and discrimination.

Herf reminds us of the one constant – other than hatred of Jews – that applies to all antisemites, whichever end of the political or religious spectrum they come from: they suffer from no surfeit of reason. Antisemitism is an absurd, illogical and irrational animus, one that, but for the terrible damage it inflicts, should be the source of disdainful laughter, ridicule and wickedly clever jokes. Jews, of course, have long made those jokes – and sadly, given contemporary conditions, will continue to find this dark humour necessary. This might be a good place to note the definition of a Jewish telegram: "Start worrying. Details to follow."

*Deborah E. Lipstadt is the Dorot Professor of Modern Jewish History and Holocaust Studies at Emory University.*

www.ingramcontent.com/pod-product-compliance
Lightning Source LLC
Chambersburg PA
CBHW021014160726
47994CB00006B/2502